The **Essential** Buyer's Guide

MERCEDES-BENZ
S-CLASS
W126-series 1979-1991

Your marque expert:
Tobias Zoporowski

VELOCE PUBLISHING
THE PUBLISHER OF FINE AUTOMOTIVE BOOKS

Essential Buyer's Guide Series

Alfa Romeo Alfasud (Metcalfe)
Alfa Romeo Alfetta: all saloon/sedan models 1972 to 1984 & coupé models 1974 to 1987 (Metcalfe)
Alfa Romeo Giulia GT Coupé (Booker)
Alfa Romeo Giulia Spider (Booker)
Audi TT (Davies)
Audi TT Mk2 2006 to 2014 (Durnan)
Austin-Healey Big Healeys (Trummel)
BMW Boxer Twins (Henshaw)
BMW E30 3 Series 1981 to 1994 (Hosier)
BMW GS (Henshaw)
BMW X5 (Saunders)
BMW Z3 Roadster (Fishwick)
BMW Z4: E85 Roadster and E86 Coupé including M and Alpina 2003 to 2009 (Smitheram)
BSA 350, 441 & 500 Singles (Henshaw)
BSA 500 & 650 Twins (Henshaw)
BSA Bantam (Henshaw)
Choosing, Using & Maintaining Your Electric Bicycle (Henshaw)
Citroën 2CV (Paxton)
Citroën ID & DS (Heilig)
Cobra Replicas (Ayre)
Corvette C2 Sting Ray 1963-1967 (Falconer)
Datsun 240Z 1969 to 1973 (Newlyn)
DeLorean DMC-12 1981 to 1983 (Williams)
Ducati Bevel Twins (Falloon)
Ducati Desmodue Twins (Falloon)
Ducati Desmoquattro Twins – 851, 888, 916, 996, 998, ST4 1988 to 2004 (Falloon)
Fiat 500 & 600 (Bobbitt)
Ford Capri (Paxton)
Ford Escort Mk1 & Mk2 (Williamson)
Ford Model A – All Models 1927 to 1931 (Buckley)
Ford Model T – All models 1909 to 1927 (Barker)
Ford Mustang – First Generation 1964 to 1973 (Cook)
Ford Mustang (Cook)
Ford RS Cosworth Sierra & Escort (Williamson)
Harley-Davidson Big Twins (Henshaw)
Hillman Imp (Morgan)
Hinckley Triumph triples & fours 750, 900, 955, 1000, 1050, 1200 – 1991-2009 (Henshaw)
Honda CBR FireBlade (Henshaw)
Honda CBR600 Hurricane (Henshaw)
Honda SOHC Fours 1969-1984 (Henshaw)
Jaguar E-Type 3.8 & 4.2 litre (Crespin)
Jaguar E-type V12 5.3 litre (Crespin)

Jaguar Mark 1 & 2 (All models including Daimler 2.5-litre V8) 1955 to 1969 (Thorley)
Jaguar New XK 2005-2014 (Thorley)
Jaguar S-Type – 1999 to 2007 (Thorley)
Jaguar X-Type – 2001 to 2009 (Thorley)
Jaguar XJ-S (Crespin)
Jaguar XJ6, XJ8 & XJR (Thorley)
Jaguar XK 120, 140 & 150 (Thorley)
Jaguar XK8 & XKR (1996-2005) (Thorley)
Jaguar/Daimler XJ 1994-2003 (Crespin)
Jaguar/Daimler XJ40 (Crespin)
Jaguar/Daimler XJ6, XJ12 & Sovereign (Crespin)
Kawasaki Z1 & Z900 (Orritt)
Land Rover Discovery Series 1 (1989-1998) (Taylor)
Land Rover Discovery Series 2 (1998-2004) (Taylor)
Land Rover Series I, II & IIA (Thurman)
Land Rover Series III (Thurman)
Lotus Elan, S1 to Sprint and Plus 2 to Plus 2S 130/5 1962 to 1974 (Vale)
Lotus Europa, S1, S2, Twin-cam & Special 1966 to 1975 (Vale)
Lotus Seven replicas & Caterham 7: 1973-2013 (Hawkins)
Mazda MX-5 Miata (Mk1 1989-97 & Mk2 98-2001) (Crook)
Mazda RX-8 (Parish)
Mercedes Benz Pagoda 230SL, 250SL & 280SL roadsters & coupés (Bass)
Mercedes-Benz 190: all 190 models (W201 series) 1982 to 1993 (Parish)
Mercedes-Benz 280-560SL & SLC (Bass)
Mercedes-Benz SL R129-series 1989 to 2001 (Parish)
Mercedes-Benz SLK (Bass)
Mercedes-Benz W123 (Parish)
Mercedes-Benz W124 – All models 1984-1997 (Zoporowski)
MG Midget & A-H Sprite (Horler)
MG TD, TF & TF1500 (Jones)
MGA 1955-1962 (Crosier)
MGB & MGB GT (Williams)
MGF & MG TF (Hawkins)
Mini (Paxton)
Morris Minor & 1000 (Newell)
Moto Guzzi 2-valve big twins (Falloon)
New Mini (Collins)
Norton Commando (Henshaw)
Peugeot 205 GTI (Blackburn)
Piaggio Scooters – all modern two-stroke & four-stroke automatic models 1991 to 2016 (Willis)

Porsche 356 (Johnson)
Porsche 911 (964) (Streather)
Porsche 911 (993) (Streather)
Porsche 911 (996) (Streather)
Porsche 911 (997) – Model years 2004 to 2009 (Streather)
Porsche 911 (997) – Second generation models 2009 to 2012 (Streather)
Porsche 911 Carrera 3.2 (Streather)
Porsche 911SC (Streather)
Porsche 924 – All models 1976 to 1988 (Hodgkins)
Porsche 928 (Hemmings)
Porsche 930 Turbo & 911 (930) Turbo (Streather)
Porsche 944 (Higgins)
Porsche 981 Boxster & Cayman (Streather)
Porsche 986 Boxster (Streather)
Porsche 987 Boxster and Cayman 1st generation (2005-2009) (Streather)
Porsche 987 Boxster and Cayman 2nd generation (2009-2012) (Streather)
Range Rover – First Generation models 1970 to 1996 (Taylor)
Range Rover – Second Generation 1994-2001 (Taylor)
Rolls-Royce Silver Shadow & Bentley T-Series (Bobbitt)
Royal Enfield Bullet (Henshaw)
Subaru Impreza (Hobbs)
Sunbeam Alpine (Barker)
Triumph 350 & 500 Twins (Henshaw)
Triumph Bonneville (Henshaw)
Triumph Stag (Mort)
Triumph Thunderbird, Trophy & Tiger (Henshaw)
Triumph TR2 & TR3 - All models (including 3A & 3B) 1953 to 1962 (Conners)
Triumph TR4/4A & TR5/250 - All models 1961 to 1968 (Child & Battyll)
Triumph TR6 (Williams)
Triumph TR7 & TR8 (Williams)
Triumph Trident & BSA Rocket III (Rooke)
TVR S-series (Kitchen)
Velocette 350 & 500 Singles 1946 to 1970 (Henshaw)
Vespa Scooters – Classic 2-stroke models 1960-2008 (Paxton)
Volkswagen Bus (Copping)
Volvo 700/900 Series (Beavis)
Volvo P1800/1800S, E & ES 1961 to 1973 (Murray)
VW Beetle (Copping)
VW Golf GTI (Copping)

www.veloce.co.uk

Original German edition first published by Heel Verlag-GmbH, Gut Pottscheidt, 53639, Konigswinter, Germany under the title Mercedes-Benz S-Klasse (W126) Alle Modelle von 1979-1991.

This English translation first published in February 2019 by Veloce Publishing Limited, Veloce House, Parkway Farm Business Park, Middle Farm Way, Poundbury, Dorchester, Dorset, DT1 3AR, England. Tel +44 (0)1305 260068/Fax 01305 250479/ e-mail info@veloce.co.uk or www.velocebooks.com.

ISBN: 978-1-787114-02-9 UPC: 6-36847-01402-5

Readers with ideas for automotive books, or books on other transport or related hobby subjects, are invited to write to the editorial director of Veloce Publishing at the above address.

British Library Cataloguing in Publication Data – A catalogue record for this book is available from the British Library.

Typesetting, design and page make-up all by Veloce Publishing Ltd on Apple Mac. Printed and bound in India by Replika Press.

W126 – the king of the three-pointed star

The 126-series' predecessor, the W116 – still laden with chrome trim – had already been honoured with the title of 'The best car in the world,' bestowed on it by the motoring press and numerous experts at the time, and scarcely questioned since. As progress should be a one-way street, the manufacturer's wish was that the W126, introduced in 1979, should take up the baton. This it duly did: for many enthusiasts, the W126 remains to this day the best – and above all the most elegant and confidently styled – S-Class Mercedes-Benz ever built. It was dignified without being arrogant, stately but never garish. The exceptionally coherent and intrinsically soothing design of its bodywork, which has come through the decades without becoming old-fashioned, was the responsibility of none other than Bruno Sacco, the company's head of design, sometimes referred to as 'The master of timelessness.'

Of course, it was not only its remarkably long-lasting design that accounted for the success of the Stuttgart limo. Mercedes' top model, latterly known as the S-Class, always demonstrated the company's latest technology, and for the 126-series that was especially the case, with the first extensive use of electronics. At the beginning of the 1980s, assistance systems such as pyrotechnic seatbelt pretensioners, and driver and passenger airbags (from 1981 and 1987 respectively), together with ABS brakes and a traction control system (ASR) were as innovative as they were expensive, and only became available in Mercedes' smaller models considerably later.

Clockwise from above: early 126s can be recognised by their ribbed side mouldings. They have an appeal all of their own. With 14-inch wheels and without a passenger door mirror, the imposing saloon is charmingly middle-class.

The creator and his work: chief designer Bruno Sacco with a model of the C126. Many fans consider the magnificent coupé his greatest success.

At the start of the eighties, buyers were still daring: nobody was offended by an S-Class finished in a gaudy yellow.
(All pictures courtesy Mercedes-Benz AG)

At that time, it was almost impossible to predict the use of technology which is as much a part of any car today as its four wheels, particularly with regard to its long-term durability. Mercedes itself recommended that the airbags be replaced every 10-15 years on safety grounds. This recommendation was later officially dropped, and the author is unaware of any cars in which the airbags fitted when new have been replaced without any particular reason. Faults with the ABS and ASR control units do occur as the cars age, but not in any significant numbers.

In the view of many enthusiasts, in this respect the S-Class combines exactly those factors which have always allowed every Mercedes to mature into a classic: styling which was just behind the cutting edge of fashion, state-of-the-art driving safety and comfort, and excellent build quality, so that it would simply carry on working for many years. With a well-cared for W126 you can still look well-dressed even today, regardless of whether you park it in front of the Four Seasons Hotel in a large city or at a discount store.

Even after 24 years, there is still a wide choice of engines, colours and equipment, and all the petrol-engined cars are refined to drive. The coupé is only available with V8 engines, while the sole diesel – the 300 SDL, which was sold only in North America – is not really in keeping with the car's status. But if you are into unusual models and aren't put off by the horrendous running costs, you may strike lucky with one of these rare versions.

Before you set off on the hunt for your W126, however, you should be aware that an S-Class is never really cheap. It wasn't when it was new, and it isn't today. To purchase and maintain a W126 in decent condition you need to keep some cash in reserve. Beware of supposed bargains on the internet, it's been a long time since there have been trouble-free S-Classes for less than ⬤x3000! Take the time to ready this Buyer's Guide thoroughly, consult specialist publications and make contacts in the active enthusiast community. With a little patience, the king of the three-pointed star may soon have its place in your garage.

Vision and reality: at the Frankfurt Motor Show in 1981, Mercedes-Benz presented the 'Auto 2000' concept car based on the 126-series. It took up the essential design characteristics of the S-Class and served as a technological showcase for features such as its safety equipment. The complete front-end of the car, for example, was made from a plastic developed specially by Bayer (known as 'Soft Nose'). (Courtesy Mercedes-Benz AG)

The S-Class in its most beautiful form: the C126 coupé is both gracious and majestic. The story goes that Bruno Sacco disliked the plastic trim behind the door handles, which he felt was incongruous. (Courtesy Mercedes-Benz AG)

Contents

Introduction
– the purpose of this book 3

1 Is it the right car for you?
– marriage guidance 6

2 Cost considerations
– affordable, or a money pit? 9

3 Living with a W126
– will you get along together? 11

4 Relative values
– which model for you? 12

5 Before you view
– be well informed 18

6 Inspection equipment
– these items will really help 21

7 Fifteen minute evaluation
– walk away or stay? 22

8 Key points
– where to look for problems 28

9 Serious evaluation
– 60 minutes for years of
   enjoyment....................................30

10 Auctions
– sold! Another way to buy your
   dream..44

11 Paperwork
– correct documentation is
   essential! 46

12 What's it worth?
– let your head rule your heart! 48

13 Do you really want to restore?
– it'll take longer and cost more
   than you think..............................52

14 Paint problems
– a bad complexion, including
   dimples, pimples and bubbles 54

15 Problems due to lack of use
– just like their owners, W126s
   need exercise 56

16 The Community
– key people, organisations and
   companies in the Mercedes world
  59

17 Vital statistics
– essential data at your fingertips.....61

The Essential Buyer's Guide™ currency
At the time of publication a BG unit of currency " ● " equals approximately £1.00/US$1.28/Euro 1.13. Please adjust to suit current exchange rates using Sterling as the base currency.

1 Is it the right car for you?
– marriage guidance

Suitability for everyday use
Every W126 Mercedes remains eminently suitable for everyday use, provided it has been regularly serviced and maintained. With one minor reservation: models not fitted with a catalytic converter will not obtain the windscreen sticker needed to enter city centres in some countries. The only solution in such cases is to register the car as a historic vehicle (where such schemes exist) or retrofit a catalytic converter.

This W126 has 250,000 miles on the clock, thanks to careful maintenance, but can still be used every day. (Courtesy S Mantel)

Interior space
There is enough room in both the saloon and coupé for at least four adults and their luggage. Even tall drivers should have no problems. The coupé is a strict four-seater; the two separate rear seats were an option on the saloon at extra cost.

Ease of use
Power assistance, together with the large, ship-like steering wheel, ensures the steering is light to use. If you are new to Mercedes, once you have become accustomed to the foot-operated parking brake, driving a W126 holds few secrets. All the warning lights, instruments and switches are self-explanatory; even the controls on highly-equipped models won't overwhelm the driver. This is also due to the fact that Mercedes would not sanction the fitting of any blank switches on the S-Class: the number of controls on the centre console corresponds exactly to the equipment fitted.

The luxurious red leather has an appeal of its own. The leather upholstery fitted to the first series of cars is considered particularly durable. (Courtesy S Mantel)

Luggage space
Both the saloon and coupé offer generously sized, well-lit luggage compartments. There is, however, no through-load facility to the interior of the car.

Will it fit in the garage?
Even a 'standard,' short-wheelbase W126 measures a full five metres (well over 16ft)

The electrical convenience features (here the seat memory) should be thoroughly checked. (Courtesy Mercedes-Benz AG)

in length. It should fit most standard garages. The long-wheelbase versions are nearly 5.20m (17ft) long, so you will probably need to drive the car right up to the front wall for the door to close without difficulty. At just over 1.8m (nearly 6ft) wide, however, the W126 is noticeably narrower than its modern successors, so it should be possible to open the doors of the saloon in a regular garage without any problems. It may be a tighter fit, though, with the long front doors of the coupés.

Running costs

Service and running costs for a W126 naturally depend to a considerable extent on the engine fitted, and in addition the earliest models were not originally fitted with a catalytic converter. If the car can be registered in your country as an historic vehicle, that may not be a problem. Nonetheless, you should always keep in mind that running an S-Class is not an inexpensive pleasure. If you use original Mercedes parts to maintain and repair it, you will pay accordingly high prices. All the engines are relatively thirsty; you should reckon on fuel consumption (gas mileage) of 20mpg (US)/24mpg (Imp) at best.

Spare parts

Ordered today, delivered tomorrow: that holds good for any Mercedes dealer and, to all intents and purposes, any part you need. Independent specialists stock a good range of parts, often of comparable quality and at much cheaper prices Many suppliers have specialised in this series and hold good stocks of used and reproduction parts. Many scrap dealers have also long specialised in the different series of Mercedes.

Insurance

You can't run an S-Class as cheaply as a VW Polo! That is the insurance companies' view as well. But if you want to use a 300 SE, for example, as a daily driver and have a good driving record, you shouldn't pay more than for a regular VW Passat. In addition, many insurers will recognise the W126 as a classic car, for which special rates apply. Be careful though: you may not be able to use the car on an everyday basis or will have to accept some conditions, such as an agreed value or limited annual mileage. You should check this with your insurer.

Investment potential
There is a clear difference in the range of cars on offer: saloons in decent condition which are still in daily use and show a few signs of wear and tear can be purchased for well under ●x9000 and should hold onto their value. Prices for very well maintained saloons and coupés with high specifications, possibly with well-known former owners, are increasing markedly. It is no longer possible to waste money on any S-Class which has a documented service history, and is without a list of jobs waiting to be done.

Plus points
There is scarcely any other car from its time which better symbolises the Federal Republic of Germany of the 1980s than the W126. In its day, it was the dominant car to be seen around government ministries. The powers that be in Germany drove – or were driven in – the S-Class. Its imperturbable air of solidity and stately bearing have always been part of its character. Its design is timeless, while its comfort, space and safety remain state of the art.

Minus points
The popularity of the W126-series means that there are many dodgy cars on the market. Don't fall for suspiciously low prices! You will never find a trouble-free one-owner S-Class for under ●x3000. The follow-up costs which a supposed bargain like this will entail can be exorbitant.

Alternatives
If you set store by the same virtues as those of the W126, but don't need as much room or status, you could turn to the W124, which has been increasing in price for some time now. Otherwise, of course, the most serious competitor to the S-Class in its day was the 7-Series BMW. At the time, it was considered the sportier and more dynamic car to drive, and in the 750i the Bavarians even offered a genuine 12-cylinder model. As a classic today, however, it is less sought after and offered, even in good condition, at almost embarrassingly low prices. Audi was something of an outsider with its 200 or the technically interesting V8 model based on it, and had yet to attain the premium status it enjoys today. Those with more exotic tastes might consider the Lexus LS400.

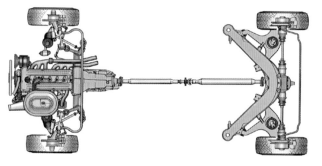

Depending on the engine and driving style, the chassis and power train of a W126 can be subjected to heavy loads. There are no problems with spare parts. (Courtesy Mercedes-Benz AG)

2 Cost considerations
– affordable, or a money pit?

It should be said from the outset that the wide range of models and engines in the 126-series means it is hard to make generalised statements about the incidental costs you may incur. A 'poverty spec' model will not trouble you with faults to electrical convenience features it doesn't have! But the picture can be very different with a fully optioned 560 SEL or SEC. If a model such as this is also equipped with hydropneumatic suspension, which can develop leaks as it ages, repairs can be painfully expensive. The cost will also vary – especially with regard to labour rates – according to whether you entrust repair and maintenance work to an official Mercedes dealer or to an independent specialist. All the prices below are for guidance only and apply to a 300 SE fitted with the M 103 engine. They include parts and labour costs as well as sales tax.

Service (minor/major), with no additional items ●x250/505
Replace accessory drivebelt and tensioners ●x684
Replace timing chain and tensioners ●x629
Replace plugs ●x71
Replace radiator ●x463
Replace water pump and thermostat ●x1020
Fit new exhaust from catalytic converter back ●x613
Replace clutch (complete) ●x1301
Replace camshaft and rocker arms ●x3039
Replace front suspension ball joints ●x479
Replace front control arms ●x1977
Replace front and rear shock absorbers ●x1125
Replace both pressure accumulators for self-levelling suspension ●x846
Replace wheel bearings (front and rear) ●x2253
Replace front and rear brake pads ●x319
Change brake fluid ●x120
Replace flexible coupling for gearbox output ●x294
Replace cylinder head gasket ●x1044
Adjust foot-operated parking brake ●x79
Perform wheel alignment check (and fit new tie rods) ●x398
Replace tilt mechanism for sunroof ●x1396
Replace engine control unit ●x1625
Replace ignition control module ●x673
Change automatic transmission fluid (ATF) ●x330
Adjust free play in steering ●x118
Replace ECU for traction control (ASR) ●x673
Repair leaks in air-conditioning, refill system and replace condenser ●x946

As a rule of thumb, electrical and electronic faults are in principle just as expensive to repair as on a modern car. Occasionally, used or replacement control units can be picked up from online auction sites amazingly cheaply. If you can't spare the money for a new component, it's worth a try, but you may be in for a surprise! As a rule, the seller won't guarantee that the part will work perfectly. Why not? Because the functions of an engine management system cannot be tested with everyday tools. As an alternative, various firms specialise in the repair of electronic control units. Often, Mercedes-Benz' official Classic Centers can also help and even provide a warranty.

This cutaway drawing shows the complexity of the W126. It is, however, relatively simple to maintain. Only repairs to specific components, such as the ECUs, prove expensive. (Courtesy Mercedes-Benz AG)

Parts that are easy to find

Basically, everything! You are driving a Mercedes, after all. Which means: everything that the car needs – or might need – to keep on running is available straight away or within 24 hours from your dealer's parts department. For parts that are subject to wear, in any case.

Parts that are hard to find

This notion hardly exists when it comes to Mercedes. With the exception of interior trim parts in exotic colours – and even then, only in velour or the Alcantara-like 'Amaretta' material – you really can get hold of everything. And if finding one particular part does seem truly hopeless, you can always turn to the active clubs catering to the model. Here someone always has something or knows someone who does.

The engines can reach high mileages, but the engine and ignition control units can cause trouble and are costly to replace. Fitting used parts is not recommended, unless they come from a reputable supplier. (Courtesy Mercedes-Benz AG)

Parts that are particularly expensive

Driving an S-Class and maintaining it as it deserves generally doesn't come cheap! The optional hydropneumatic suspension can entail horrendous repair bills. On occasion, it may even be cheaper to convert the car to conventional suspension than to repair the complex hydropneumatic system. If you have fallen for one of the armoured models, you should be prepared for the fact that merely replacing one of the armour-plated side panels can cost as much as a decent small car. All the armoured cars were specially built, and hardly any parts fit off the shelf.

The exhaust systems are generally long-lasting. (Courtesy Mercedes-Benz AG)

The semi-trailing arm rear suspension ensures the car's comfort and roadholding. (Courtesy Mercedes-Benz AG)

3 Living with a W126
– will you get along together?

A Mercedes W126 is a classic the whole family can enjoy. That also applies to the coupé. The interiors of both models offer a princely amount of room, with the two-door version designed as a strict four-seater. The luggage compartment is also generous in size, even for lengthy trips.

Well looked after cars can even cope with year-round use. And why not indeed? After all, that's what they were built for! If you take care to inject wax or grease into the cavities, you should be safe for years to come. In essence, the 126-series S-Class is so down-to-earth, and such a model of German engineering that even at an advanced age it rarely suffers major problems, and keeps on doing its job reliably day in, day out.

Of course, a W126 can rust, or suffer now and then from a mechanical or technical defect. Fundamentally though, such faults never arise out of sight. The car's weak spots, whether they affect its bodywork or its mechanical components, can nearly always be repaired – the exception proves the rule – at reasonable expense, unless the car has been completely neglected. In which case, you should in general steer well clear. A complete restoration of a W126 cannot be justified. There are too many good cars on the market.

Which W126 you choose to live with will depend on your budget and your personal preferences. The coupé is a stylish summer car best suited for elegant cruising. The saloon is a smart-looking companion throughout the year. All the models were built during the cars' long production run in so many colours, and with such varied items of equipment, that you still have an almost unlimited choice today and can follow your personal taste. Whatever you like, you'll find it! Some things may just take a bit longer. Allow yourself enough time and then buy the best car you can get for your money. The author is convinced: you'll want to grow old with this car!

A car of its time: you won't often see another early 500 SE with plastic wheel trims, finished in Mimosa Yellow with Olive leather. (Courtesy D Busch)

The second series of cars are more pleasing to look at, and, above all, better equipped and better protected against corrosion. (Courtesy Mercedes-Benz AG)

First impressions: often the extent of maintenance (or lack of it) will give an indication as to the car's intrinsic worth. (Courtesy H-P Lange)

A timeless companion: a second-series SEC coupé in a fresh-looking Diamond Blue. (Courtesy H-P Lange)

11

Saloon

Timeless design marked the traditional theme of Mercedes' design department; the styling of its cars always just behind the cutting edge of fashion. And even now – regardless of the engine fitted, and especially in dark colours such as Midnight Blue (code 904) – it still looks imposing and most respectable: the best possible basis for describing it as a 'classic.' A wide range of cars are still on the road, more or less well preserved, and with every possible combination of colour and equipment. The saloon is also the only model in the range to have been offered with all the engines, from the carburettor-fed 280 S to the 560 SEL, with its beefy V8 and long-wheelbase.

Coupé

Many fans of this series consider the glamorous coupé to be quite simply its creator Bruno Sacco's masterpiece, and therefore one of the most attractive and best-resolved luxury cars of the 1980s. The two-door model was offered only with V8 engines and as a strict four-seater. As a result, the coupé provides graceful and comfortable transport for four adults, even for long journeys. It is characterised by its side profile with no B-pillar. When all the windows are open – even the rear side windows can be fully lowered – it almost feels like a convertible. To save the driver and front seat passenger from straining themselves, after getting in and turning on the ignition, a plastic arm whirrs forward to present the seatbelt. It is essential that this curious-looking but extremely helpful electrical aid should be in working order! Replacements are expensive. Over the years, many coupés have become the victims of customising. Shorter, stiffer sets of springs and shock absorbers or excessively wide tyres put an

A classic Mercedes PR shot: a saloon with cherry blossom behind it. The clothes give away when the picture was taken, but the S-Class still looks modern. (Courtesy Mercedes-Benz AG)

The side windows on the coupé go all the way down, giving the car an airy appearance and the feel of a convertible inside. (Courtesy Mercedes-Benz AG)

Mercedes never produced an official 126-series convertible, but you might want to consider a six-cylinder A124. (Courtesy Mercedes-Benz Classic)

extra load on the complex suspension. You should avoid cars such as these, including models which have obviously been restored to standard specification, even if the price is temptingly low.

Petrol or diesel?

First, it should be said that the W126 was never officially offered in Europe with diesel engines; the only version was for the North American market (US and Canada). The 300 SDL was fitted with an in-line six-cylinder engine developing 150bhp. Cars which have been exported back to Europe can immediately be identified by their much bulkier front and rear bumpers (fenders) and sealed-beam headlamps, which will have to be converted for use in Europe. In addition, North American models fitted with automatic transmission do not have a programme selector (S/E). In Europe, big diesel engines like this without any emissions controls are either highly taxed or face increasing restrictions on their use in urban areas, with the result that the number of S-Class diesels is exceedingly small. If you are looking for something out of the ordinary – and succeed in finding a car – you may strike lucky. In terms of its driving characteristics, however, an SDL can hardly be recommended.

The petrol engines on the other hand – six- and eight-cylinder versions exist – are all tough and long-lived. Connoisseurs like the early 280 SE (M 110) for its sparkling performance and flexibility, but the carburettor version (280 S) has all but disappeared. For the second series (or face-lifted models) sold from 1985 onwards, Mercedes borrowed the 2.6-litre M 103 engine developing 158 bhp from the W124 range, and fitted it to its new entry-level model, the 260 SE. Given the car's high weight, this appeared somewhat overstretched. As a laid-back cruiser, however, and with no expectation that the car will be a sprinter, it is not a bad choice. The high-volume

The 300 SD Diesel was produced only for North America; in Europe it is extremely rare, and little sought after. (Courtesy Mercedes-Benz AG)

Starter-level S-Class: many buyers of the smallest-engined cars chose the 'delete badge' option, but the first owner of this car stood by their decision. And why not? The 158bhp six-cylinder was always sufficient to ensure relaxed cruising. (Courtesy S Mantel)

A V8, German-style: the 5-litre is a brawny, powerful unit and could almost be considered economical. (Courtesy Mercedes-Benz AG)

In a dark colour, the stately S-Class could be seen throughout the world as the car of ministers and ambassadors. Even now, it still looks dignified and highly respectable. (Courtesy H-P Lange)

The lines of the W126 make it appear handsome from any angle. (Courtesy H-P Lange)

The 'small' V8 from the first series (380 SE) is now rare, but it is a refined car to drive.

Cars in such exceptional condition are seldom sold privately. This one was for sale at Techno Classica Essen in 2014 with a five-figure price tag.

model in the range, the 300 SE (M 103), producing 177bhp, offers a noticeably better combination of performance and economy. It remains very common today and there is an excellent chance of acquiring a 300 SE at a reasonable price.

Back in the day, the 500 and 560 SE/SEC with their M 117 V8 engines were considered dream cars. Their magnificently powerful, smooth and refined power delivery in all conditions was unmatched at the time, and remains desirable today. The performance delivered by the 560's engines – which produced up to 275bhp (for the versions equipped with a catalytic converter) – has nothing to fear from any modern competitors. Pride of place goes to the non-catalysed 'ECE' version of this engine, which developed a full 296bhp. That is quite an experience, if you have the budget to enjoy it. There is a considerable difference in personality between the 500 and 560 models, due to their different rear axle ratios. Owners who enjoy a relaxed drive favour the 500: thanks to its longer gearing, this runs at lower revs throughout the speed range and is quieter. The 560, on the other hand, comes across as a sports car engine and thrives on revs. Which you prefer is a matter of personal taste. The eight-cylinder engines are good for high mileages, thanks to the relatively low thermal and mechanical loads to which they are subject. Cars which have covered 300,000 miles or more are commonplace, and by no means exceptional. In order to reach these high mileages, it is worth taking regular care of the duplex (or twin-row) timing chain and its tensioners, together with the camshaft and rocker arms. By 'taking care' of them we mean having the engine opened up by a specialist and the condition of these components checked and, where appropriate, replaced. Owners in the know advise this precautionary measure after covering about 150,000 miles.

The two 'small' V8s in the 380 SE/SEL/SEC (until 1985) and 420 SE/SEL/SEC (from 1985, engine type M 116) should not be overlooked. When new, they were considerably cheaper than the larger-engined versions, although they were not fitted with the anti-squat geometry which came as standard on the 500 and 560 SE/

An S-Class, especially a glamorous 500 SEC, looks particularly good with a celebrity owner such as F1 legend Ayrton Senna, seen here with his coupé. (Courtesy Mercedes-Benz AG)

Plenty of space: the standard-wheelbase saloon was by some margin the most widely sold version. Its passengers did not suffer from any shortage of space. (Courtesy D Busch)

High society: a long-wheelbase S-Class should really be driven by a chauffeur. (Courtesy Mercedes-Benz AG)

Showing its best side: from this angle the side profile of the SEC is particularly successful. (Courtesy Mercedes-Benz AG)

SEL/SEC and prevented the rear of the car from dipping when accelerating. Apart from their slightly more modest performance, both these engines are just as refined and powerful. Nowadays, however, both models are surprisingly rare.

Face-lift or new series?

Whichever expression you prefer – purists prefer the term 'series' – the W126 can be divided into two phases of development: the first series, produced from 1979-1985, and the second series (or face-lifted models), built from 1985-1991. Many W126 enthusiasts consider the latter the more elegant and attractive versions, thanks, not least, to the cosmetic changes which Mercedes made to the first generation. The side mouldings (sometimes called 'Sacco panels'), which had previously been finished in a contrasting colour and had a ribbed texture, now had a smooth surface and could be ordered in colours to match the bodywork. Together with the revised, deeper front apron, the subtly restyled window frames and the switch to 15-inch wheels (for both steel and alloy rims), the big cars looked altogether sleeker and more modern.

Inside too, there were minor changes, with a modified rear seat and some alterations to the control layout: some switches, for example, moved from the dashboard to the roof panel.

The biggest changes, however, were to be found under the bonnet (hood): apart from the 5-litre V8, all the power units were updated and were immediately available with three-way catalytic converters or, if preferred, in so-called 'RÜF' versions which could later be retrofitted with a converter.

The blessing of the W126 cars' early development was that both series were spared the serious corrosion problems which beset large numbers of the final W124-series cars. Mercedes only switched its paint lines to use the initially

At full speed: even now a W126 feels right at home on the motorway or freeway. It is scarcely possible to travel in greater comfort. (Courtesy Mercedes-Benz AG)

problematic water-based paints in 1993, two years after production of the 126-series came to an end.

Relative values

Find the current value in your country of one of the models listed here at 100%, such as the popular 280 SE or 300

Officially approved three-way catalytic converters were available with all engines from the second series (1985) onwards, or could be retrofitted to the 'RÜF' versions. (Courtesy Mercedes-Benz AG)

SE, using the various published and online valuation guides. Then use the relative value column to estimate the value of the other models.

W126 petrol-engined saloons

Model	Production years	Bhp	Cc	Relative value
260 SE Cat	1986-1991	158	2548	100%
280 S	1979-1985	154	2746	90%
280 SE	1979-1985	182	2746	100%
280 SEL	1979-1985	182	2746	100%
300 SE	1985-1987	185	2962	100%
300 SE Cat	1987-1991	177	2962	100%
300 SEL	1985-1991	185	2962	100%
300 SEL Cat	1985-1991	177	2962	110%
380 SE	1979-1985	215/201 (from 10/81)	3818/3839 (from 10/81)	110%
380 SEL	1979-1985	215/201 (from 10/81)	3818/3839 (from 10/81)	110%
420 SE Cat	1985-1991	215	4196	110%
420 SEL Cat	1987-1991	221	4196	110%
500 SE	1979-1985	237	4973	130%
500 SE Cat	1985-1987	220	4973	120%
500 SE Cat	1987-1991	249	4973	120%
500 SEL	1980-1985	228	4973	130%
500 SEL	1987-1991	228	4973	130%
500 SEL Cat	1986-1991	220	4973	130%
560 SE	1985-1992	275	5547	150%
560 SEL	1986-1989	295	5547	160%

Model	Production years	Bhp	Cc	Relative value
380 SEC	1981-1985	201	3839	110%
420 SEC	1985-1987	215	4196	100%
420 SEC Cat	1987-1991	221	4196	100%
500 SEC	1981-1985	228	4973	120%
500 SEC	1985-1991	249	4973	120%
560 SEC	1985-1987	296	5547	140%
560 SEC Cat	1987-1991	275	5547	140%

Cat = car fitted with catalytic converter

The police in Baden-Württemberg used a few S-Classes during the 1980s and they remained in service for a long time. Several of them were fitted with armour-plating and used as escort vehicles by the state government. (Courtesy Mercedes-Benz AG)

5 Before you view
– be well informed

To avoid a wasted journey, and the disappointment of finding that the car does not match your expectations, it will help if you're very clear about what questions you want to ask before you pick up the telephone. Some of these points might appear basic, but when you're excited about the prospect of buying your dream classic, it's amazing how some of the most obvious things slip the mind ... You can also check the current values of the model which attracts you in classic car magazines, which give both a price guide and auction results.

Where is the car?
Is it going to be worth travelling to the next county/state, or even across a border? A locally advertised car, although it may not sound very interesting, can add to your knowledge for very little effort, so make a visit – it might even be in better condition than expected.

Dealer or private sale
Establish early on if the car is being sold by its owner or by a trader. A private owner should have all the history, so don't be afraid to ask detailed questions. A dealer may have more limited knowledge of a car's history, but should have some documentation. A dealer may offer a warranty/guarantee (ask for a printed copy) and finance.

Cost of collection and delivery
A dealer may well be used to quoting for delivery by car transporter. A private owner may agree to meet you halfway, but only agree to this after you have seen the car at the vendor's address to validate the documents. Alternatively, you could meet halfway and agree the sale but insist on meeting at the vendor's address for the handover.

View – when and where
It is always preferable to view at the vendor's home or business premises. In the case of a private sale, the car's documentation should tally with the vendor's name and address. Arrange to view only in daylight and avoid a wet day. Most cars look better in poor light or when wet.

Reason for sale
Do make it one of the first questions. Why is the car being sold and how long has it been with the current owner? How many previous owners?

Imports
There are usually plenty of W126 saloons and coupés on sale in Germany and if left-hand drive is not an issue, you may want to extend your search there. When you buy a car from another country, you may need to make changes to the number (licence) plates, lighting (headlamps and indicators) and radio equipment. If you re-register a car from Germany or another country, you may need to obtain an attestation from Mercedes-Benz that it conforms to the original specification. Take

particular care if you are considering buying a car first registered in Japan which has later been exported to Europe or North America, as the original Japanese specification may not meet requirements in your market.

Condition (body/chassis/interior/mechanicals)

Query the car's condition in as specific terms as possible – preferably citing the checklist items described in Chapter 9.

All-original specification

With the exception of the now rare conversions carried out in period by companies such as AMG or Brabus, an original equipment car is invariably of higher value than a customised version. Beware of cars which have been lowered or fitted with extra-wide wheels, which are ill-suited to the W126's complex suspension.

Matching data/legal ownership

Do Vehicle Identification Number (VIN)/ chassis, engine numbers and licence plate match the official registration document? Is the owner's name and address recorded in the official registration documents? For those countries that require an annual test of roadworthiness, does the car have a document showing it complies (an MoT certificate in the UK, which can be verified on www.gov.uk/check-mot-status)? If a smog/ emissions certificate is mandatory, does the car have one? If required, does the car carry a current road fund licence/ licence plate tag? Does the vendor own the car outright? Money might be

Somewhat shabby-looking cars like this have an appeal of their own for some would-be buyers. If you have the technical skill and know what you are taking on, they can be good projects. (Courtesy H-P Lange)

You could also buy a car which has been modified. But have all the changes been properly approved?

The advantage of buying a car from a dealer specialising in classics: for the most part, a guarantee is provided. As a result, the price is often considerably higher.

owed to a finance company or bank: the car could even be stolen. Several organisations will supply the data on ownership, based on the car's licence plate number, for a fee. Such companies can often also tell you whether the car has been 'written-off' by an insurance company. In the UK, the following organisations can supply vehicle data:

HPI – 0845 300 8905; www.hpi.co.uk/
AA – 0800 316 3564; http://www.theaa.com/vehicle-check
DVLA – 0300 790 6802; www.gov.uk/get-vehicle-information-from-dvla/
RAC – 0330 159 0364; https://vehicle-history-check.rac.co.uk/
Other countries will have similar organisations.

Insurance
Check with your existing insurer before setting out, your current policy might not cover you to drive the car if you do purchase it.

How you can pay
A cheque (check) will take several days to clear and the seller may prefer to sell to a cash buyer. However, a banker's draft (a cheque issued by a bank) is as good as cash, but safer, so contact your own bank and become familiar with the formalities that are necessary to obtain one.

Buying at auction?
If your intention is to buy at auction, see Chapter 10 for further advice.

Professional vehicle check (mechanical examination)
There are often marque/model specialists who will undertake professional examination of a vehicle on your behalf. Owners' clubs will be able to put you in touch with such specialists. Other motoring organisations with vehicle inspectors that will carry out a general professional check in the UK are:

AA – 0800 056 8040; www.theaa.com/
RAC – 0330 159 0324/0720; www.rac.co.uk/
Other countries will have similar organisations.

6 Inspection equipment
– these items will really help

This book
Reading glasses (if you need them for close work)
Magnet (not powerful, a fridge magnet is ideal)
Torch
Probe (a small screwdriver works very well)
Overalls
Mirror on a stick
Digital camera
A friend, preferably a knowledgeable enthusiast

Before you rush out of the door, gather together a few items that will help as you work your way around the car. This book is designed to be your guide at every step, so take it along and use the check boxes to help you assess each area of the car you're interested in. Don't be afraid to let the seller see you using it.

Take your reading glasses if you need them to read documents and make close up inspections. A magnet will help you check if the car is full of filler or has fibreglass panels. Use the magnet to sample bodywork areas all around the car but be careful not to damage the paintwork. Expect to find a little filler here and there, but not whole panels. There's nothing wrong with fibreglass panels, but a purist might want the car to be as original as possible.

A torch with fresh batteries will be useful for peering into the wheel arches and under the car. A small screwdriver can be used – with care – as a probe, particularly in the wheelarches and on the underside. With this you should be able to check an area of severe corrosion but be careful – if it's really bad the screwdriver might go right through the metal!

Be prepared to get dirty. Take along a pair of overalls, if you have them. Fixing a mirror at an angle on the end of a stick may seem odd, but you'll probably need it to check the condition of the underside of the car. It will also help you to peer into some of the important crevices. You can also use it, together with the torch, along the underside of the sills and on the floor.

If you have the use of a digital camera, take it along so that later you can study some areas of the car more closely. Take a picture of any part of the car that causes you concern and seek a friend's opinion.

Ideally, have a friend or knowledgeable enthusiast accompany you: a second opinion is always valuable.

7 Fifteen minute evaluation
– walk away or stay?

In just a quarter of an hour, you won't be able to assess whether the car you are considering is really the 'friend for life' you have been looking for. Some faults go unseen by even the most honest sellers or the smartest would-be buyers, while others creep up unnoticed. After all, we are talking here about a car that on average is well over 25 years old. You would do well never to assume that it is in perfect condition, especially if it is described in those terms. The checklist that follows will at least give you some indication as to whether a more extensive examination is justified.

Bodywork
It should be obvious that you should always view a car in dry – and if possible sunny – weather. Only then will you be able to see quickly whether the car has been partially or completely repainted. When the car left the factory, there were no differences in colour – however small – between the doors, wings (fenders) and bonnet! Nor were there wide or uneven panel gaps. Minor scrapes on the plastic bumpers, side cladding or valance panels may be tolerated as the 'battle scars' of a car which is used every day. If, on the other hand, these body parts are cracked, broken or noticeably distorted, you should investigate the matter thoroughly. It is possible that real and much more serious damage is hidden behind them.

Next, it makes sense to turn to the potential rust spots. Take a look first at all four jacking points. On face-lifted cars, on the lower part of the side mouldings at sill height you will find four plastic covers, which you can carefully open up with a key or a flat-bladed screwdriver. On first-series cars, the jacking points are freely accessible and can be examined right away. If the jacking points already show clear signs of corrosion, you can safely assume that the sills are also rusting. Unless you know an expert welder, you can conclude your examination of the car at this point. Even though sheet metal for repairs is available in different grades and at varying prices, the repair will be a time-consuming job and will prove expensive. Even supposed specialists

There is sure to be a reason for misalignment of the front and rear doors: try to track it down.

This corner has taken a bit of a scrape. Ideally, the damage should be purely cosmetic.

The blistering on the left front wing does not augur well. To play it safe, the entire wing should be replaced.

The condition of the jacking points is a good indicator. On cars from the first series, they are easily accessible, with no faults apparent on this car.

Left: that little prang (see page 22) wasn't quite so minor: the bumper has clearly been pushed back towards the wheelarch. It will require straightening out and repainting, at least.

Right: corrosion on the rear wheelarch. It looks quite innocuous, but in the worst case, the entire side panel may be affected.

sometimes simply weld up the jacking points altogether. Steer well clear of any half-baked botch-ups like this! If the edges of the front wings (especially where the wing meets the front bumper), and/or the rear wheelarches (or the angled section just ahead of them) are already blistering, it will quickly be obvious. The chrome wheelarch trims which were relatively common in the 1980s should make you doubtful: the wheelarches will often be rotten underneath. The rear wheelarches were always fitted with a plastic liner when the cars were built. If this is missing, water can splash up behind the side sections and begin its nefarious work behind the carpet covering the side panels in the boot. If the luggage compartment is suspiciously damp or smells musty, that should always make you wary and you should carefully remove the carpeting at the side. The bottoms of the doors and the doorframes (lift up the door seals!), as well as the boot lid and the windscreen and rear window surrounds should all be inspected. Carrying out a professional repair to a shabby rear screen frame is particularly time-consuming and expensive. If the car you have chosen has a sunroof, look at the frame from inside and outside (are the drainage channels clear?) and, above all, check that it works! If the paint on the sunroof is scratched, this may be due to an earlier fault or a badly adjusted tilt mechanism. If the roof will not function at all, a defect of this kind – or less commonly a drive mechanism which no longer works – is very likely the cause. Many owners shy away from this kind of repair and simply get their garage to leave the roof permanently closed. If there is a distinct creaking sound when opening

The screen frames and screen edges are critical points to check. If the edges have begun to go milky, the screen is letting in water, and may not pass a safety inspection.

Checking underneath the rear screen frame is essential. If rust has set in below the rear parcel shelf, cleaning it out will be labour-intensive and costly.

Creaking door straps are a well-known problem on the rear doors of saloons, and should not be ignored.

or closing the doors – the rear doors on the saloons are particularly affected – the retaining straps have usually had it. This is a repair job which is all too often postponed, but you shouldn't wait too long to deal with it: at some point the door may jam and you will be unable to open it.

If you get the opportunity to put the car on a lift or over an inspection pit, take the chance to examine it from underneath. Take a look, preferably with a

The first coil of the front springs frequently breaks without being noticed, which will fail a roadworthiness inspection on safety grounds. You can quickly see and hear if the exhaust system is in good condition. Replacements don't come cheap, but in general last a long time.

powerful lamp, at the mounting points for the front springs and for the rear shock absorbers. Are the springs themselves in good condition? Sometimes the first coil can be broken … Cast a general eye too over all the bushings for the front and rear suspension. Naturally, all the fuel, hydraulic and brake pipes running under the car should be free from any defects, while the flexible brake hoses should not be cracked or noticeably discoloured (light grey). If the underside is conspicuously clean or has been covered with a thick layer of fresh underseal, you are right to be suspicious. You will usually notice whether the exhaust system is in good order at the same time. Finally, it does no harm to lift the bonnet and check the area around and underneath the screenwash reservoir and, if possible, the battery tray.

Interior

When you open the driver's door, the first thing you will see is the outside bolster of the driver's seat. That is all to the good, as this is often frayed or worn right through. This need not necessarily mean that the car is

You can only tell the real age of velour upholstery when it is very worn. The material used was of outstanding quality.

Left: you should lift up the carpet in the footwells to check for signs of damp. The degree of wear to the pedals also reveals a good deal about the true mileage the car has covered. Right: is the rim of the steering wheel smooth and greasy, or can you still make out the original grain of the plastic? This particular wheel has already been held for many miles, perhaps by several drivers.

The instruments and all the warning lights should work correctly. If the oil pressure gauge moves up to '3' soon after starting, all is well with the engine. A speedo needle that flutters in the first third of the speed range is acceptable, within reason. It frequently settles down when driving.

The cloth upholstery on the top of the rear seat often fades over time. This is hard to avoid, even if the car is not continually exposed to the sun.

The multi-function column stalk for the wipers and indicators is heavily used and often plays up when old. Original replacements are expensive, but good secondhand parts can be found.

Corrosion can occur around the aerial base. Here, the aerial has become stuck. Replacements are affordable.

completely worn out. Signs of wear on the pedals, gear knob and steering wheel, however, will all confirm that impression. For cars with plastic-rimmed steering wheels, is the characteristic grain of the plastic still visible or has it been rubbed smooth? For leather-rimmed wheels, how does the stitching look? Does the rim appear greasy or cracked? Does your overall impression of the interior correspond to the car's mileage and year? Are the seat cushions still reasonably firm or do they feel worn out? Are there any water stains (be sure to look under the front carpets as well!)? For cloth interiors, the sun can frequently cause fading to the rear parcel shelf or top of the rear seats, even for quite recent cars. You can either put up with it or repair it later. It needn't be a 'show-stopper' for the car in question.

Take in the appearance of the interior and check the equipment fitted. Do all the buttons and switches work? What about the heating, ventilation and air-conditioning controls, and the electric windows? Even the manual window winders can stop working, especially on the driver's door. It is also important that the sliding roof operates correctly: does it open and close quietly and reasonably quickly? Does the tilt function work? Does the wind deflector pop up and down without any problems? Look at the runners for the roof: a thorough clean and spraying them with grease has already saved many owners a costly repair job. It's almost usual to find that some of the dashboard lighting on a W126

An oil change tag with a recent date is a good indication of regular maintenance, but no guarantee that the engine is in good condition.

Unscrew the radiator cap. If the seal is distorted and wavelike, you should dispose of it. New replacements cost only around ●x5.

– whether for the main instrument panel or for the heating and ventilation controls – has stopped working. That shouldn't give cause for concern, it can be repaired by proficient home mechanics. The dashboard bulbs have plug-in sockets, and should therefore not be soldered. Other potential sources of trouble lurk in the multi-function column stalk for the indicators, main beam headlamps and windscreen wipers. Now and again the electric aerial (not available with all radios) fails to go up or down automatically. That is inconvenient, but not really a problem.

The radiator is mounted upright at the front and can easily be examined. Look out for dirt and signs of mould. Needless to say, the horn should also work.

If – like the author – you can get by without it, you can replace it with a manual aerial and put paid to the problem.

Mechanical components

Is the car still on a lift? Good. Before lowering it again, you can check the age and condition of the tyres, the universal joints and propshaft, as well as the brake discs and pads. Does everything seem satisfactory so far? If so, you can bring the car back down. Open the bonnet and check the coolant and the oil filler cap. Are there any traces of oil in the coolant reservoir, does it smell of oil or as if something has burnt? Are there signs of foam or white marks on the underside of the oil filler cap? If the answer to one of these questions is 'Yes,' you can be sure that the head gasket has failed or will do so soon. As far as you can, scour the entire cooling system for leaks. Light-coloured marks on the hoses, hose connectors or radiator may indicate places where coolant has leaked out. If there is a strong smell of petrol or diesel in the engine bay, the fuel lines may be weeping. Engines which are completely covered in oil are just as suspicious as spotless engines which have covered

This six-cylinder engine has already seen some use. That is no big deal, provided the head gasket is in good condition and all the pipes and hoses are free from leaks. The engine shouldn't look too grubby though.

200,000 miles. If the engine looks like it's been working, but shows no signs of leaks, as a rule it will be in good health.

Now is a good time to start-up the engine and listen to it running, both from a cold start and while it is operating. Does it run sweetly and without any noticeable rattling or knocking sounds? Is anything rubbing? Does the engine 'stutter' when idling? Noises from the accessory drivebelt are nothing suspicious. Even after the belt and all the tensioners have been changed, the mechanism can start squealing again after quite a short time. You just have to live with it.

If the tension is alright and the belt looks to be in good condition, as a rule you shouldn't have to worry.

During the test drive, listen carefully. Do the wheels rumble, or is there an audible noise when cornering? Either a wheel bearing is on its way out, the alignment is out or the wheels are out of balance. Nothing which can't be fixed. Or rather, you shouldn't wait too long. If the car you are considering buying is an automatic, the gears should change smoothly (the automatic gearbox is not completely jolt-free) and at the correct speeds. If you have the feeling that the transmission is taking an abnormally long time to engage the next gear, then usually something is wrong. That need not mean that the transmission is seriously damaged! Sometimes, it's enough to change the automatic transmission fluid and clean the filter element. Although many dealer workshops claim that is unnecessary, it really should be done. The car is sure to drive better afterwards.

The manual gearboxes have a reputation for being generally rather notchy, but tough. There were also considerable differences among the cars built. On some cars the manual gearshift can be very precise. Only reverse gear sometimes proves stubborn and requires a feel for it. Typically for a Mercedes, you should check the foot-operated parking brake. The pedal travel should not be too long, and it should hold the car securely on a slope without leaving the car in gear. If that is not the case, it can be adjusted, which is an inexpensive job, even in a professional workshop. Last of all, check for any free play in the steering. To some extent, it is normal for this to increase in a Mercedes which is getting on in years. But the steering should not seem excessively vague.

Do the wheels rumble, or is there an audible noise when cornering? Check the wheel bearings and suspension.

The automatic transmission should change smoothly and not take too long before engaging each gear. Changing the automatic transmission fluid from time to time can work wonders!

Some of the trouble spots on the car which are critical when assessing its condition have already been mentioned in chapter 7. Here are the key points again.

Bodywork – general

Rust in and around the jacking points weakens the overall body structure, since in most cases the sills will already be affected. Corrosion also occurs in the frames of the front and rear screens. If the edges of the glass have turned milky-white, it is almost certainly an indication that the frames are rotten. Check the bottom of each door and the window surrounds under the seals, where rust can wreak havoc undetected. It can also thrive under the side mouldings (the so-called 'Sacco panels'). If you can see rust bubbles along the upper edge of these panels, the metal underneath has usually had it. Examine the front and rear wheelarches, as well as the angled section just ahead of the rear arches, and the area where the right front wing meets the bumper. If the banana-shaped plastic liners inside the rear wheelarches are missing, it is essential to remove the carpeting and check the side panels inside the boot. Rust can develop here unseen. Check the area around the aerial base as well.

Rust around the aerial base is initially just a cosmetic issue. But water can run down into the side panel and let rust take hold there.

Front of the car

Is there any damage from stone chips on the bonnet, apron or radiator grille? Is the chrome surround of the radiator grille damaged? Are any of the plastic slats broken? Does the tongue to open the bonnet pop out okay? Is the three-pointed star present and correct, or is it crooked or broken off? How do the headlamp lenses and reflectors look? Check the resting position of the two windscreen wipers, which operate in parallel: they should drop back completely behind the edge of the bonnet.

Rear of the car

Inspect the lower edge of the boot lid and the area around the handle, lock and numberplate lights for signs of rust. Do the numberplate lights work? Is the warning triangle clipped into its mounting bracket, and the bracket itself in good condition? Is the boot damp or does it smell musty? Lift up the carpet from the boot floor and check the condition of the spare wheel well: is it bent out of shape or are there noticeable welds on the boot floor? For cars with a tow hitch, how does the electrical connector look? For those with

Corrosion readily sets in on the edge of the bootlid, around the handle, lock and number plate lights.

Cars fitted with a tow hitch may possibly have led a hard life as workhorses. Ask the last owner.

self-levelling suspension, does the rear of the car stand unnaturally high when it is unladen? If it does, the pressure accumulators may be faulty.

Engine compartment
Is the engine notably grubby or too clean for the mileage it has covered? Either situation should make you suspicious. A light film of oil around the oil filler neck is quite normal, but bigger splashes are not. Is the coolant oily or does it have a burnt smell? Is the underside of the oil filler cap frothy or sticky and whitish? If it is, it may be indicative of head gasket failure. Light-coloured stains on the cooling system hoses and the radiator itself may point to a loss of coolant. Is the sound-deadening under the bonnet in good condition, or have rodents nibbled away at it? Are all the fluid reservoirs (especially for brake fluid and the hydraulic fluid for the steering and rear differential) well filled with fresh fluid and leak-free? Is there any indication as to when the fluids were last changed? Are there any loose wires or hoses in the engine bay? (The vacuum hoses for the central locking system often slip.)

Interior
Does the condition of the interior match the year of manufacture and stated mileage of the car? Is the side bolster on the driver's seat next to the door badly worn? Is the steering wheel shiny from wear? Are the pedal rubbers and gear knob threadbare? Have the symbols on the buttons and switches been worn smooth? Does the dashboard lighting work correctly? Do the warning lights and special equipment, such as the optional trip computer or balance control for the rear speakers, all work as they should? Are there any water stains on the headlining (for cars with a sliding roof), or in the foot wells?

This interior is very smart, but leather that is not cared for develops cracks and creases, and feels rough to the touch. (Courtesy MBIG eV)

Underbody
Check the condition of all the fuel, brake and hydraulic lines. Have the brake hoses become porous?

Are the ball joints, control arms, front springs and suspension mountings free from faults? Are the rear wheel bearings and shock absorbers in good order? Is the degree of wear for the brake pads and discs (rotors), and the age and wear of the tyres still acceptable? Inspect the universal joints and propshaft. What condition are the exhaust system and catalytic converter in? Examine the overall state of the underside: is there any conspicuously thick or freshly-applied underseal (and if so, why?).

'Club Lounge': this rear seat is a nice place to spend time – when it looks as attractive as in this car. (Courtesy MBIG eV)

The complete front suspension assembly has to support a substantial weight. You should therefore check the control arms, ball joints, springs and suspension mountings. (Courtesy Mercedes-Benz AG)

9 Serious evaluation
– 60 minutes for years of enjoyment

Score each section using the boxes as follows: 4 = excellent; 3 = good; 2 = average; 1 = poor. The totting-up procedure is detailed at the end of the chapter.

Be realistic in your marking and don't let yourself be blinded by your initial excitement when you stand in front of a car which is supposedly in top condition. Keep a cool head and you'll rarely buy a pile of rubbish. Take your time and examine the car thoroughly. If you are careless and hurried, you'll often pay the price carrying out repairs afterwards. Our tip: bring a magnet, to discover areas of filler. A torch, a tyre tread depth gauge, a screwdriver, and a small mirror are also helpful.

Exterior
First impressions ☐4 ☐3 ☐2 ☐1

First of all, you should only look at a car in dry weather. Wet weather and snow will change your impression of the car's appearance enormously. If the sun is shining, better still! Then walk slowly round the car and look at it very carefully from every angle. Does the car stand level, or does it sag noticeably on one side or at one end? Is it clean and in original condition inside and out? Does the interior spell unpleasant, is it dirty or yellowed? Trust your gut feeling, first impressions are often right.

Chrome wheelarch trims should make you wary. Often the metal underneath will be rotten.

Model badges and three-pointed star emblems are popular with souvenir collectors. If you're lucky, at least the paint won't be damaged.

Corrosion on the wheelarches starts innocuously but eats away at the metal mercilessly if left untreated.
(Courtesy C Boucké)

Colours
From today's perspective, there are some pretty funny colour combinations in the 126-series. Many of them have survived, and even the

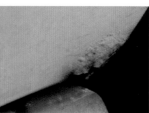

Left: this wing has almost had it ...
Right: ... rust has already attacked the entire front corner of the body. Replacing the parts is the only solution. (Both photos courtesy C Boucké)

A textbook example of a so-called 'wrong' colour: Mimosa Yellow with Olive leather, but on a 500 such an extraordinarily rare combination will have collectors licking their fingers. (All photos courtesy D Busch)

bizarre and rather over-the-top combination of Signal Red paintwork and medium-red leather upholstery won't necessarily guarantee a price reduction nowadays. Quite the opposite, in fact: the so-called 'wrong' colours, including the turquoise 'Beryl' metallic and the quite common 'Almandine' Red metallic, now have their own fans. The 1981 500 SE shown in this book finished in Mimosa Yellow with Olive leather is surrounded by people taking photographs at every club meeting. In any case, if you don't like a colour, just keep looking. There is still plenty of choice on the market.

Paintwork

For a car which is well over 25 years old, paintwork which still looks half decent is far from being in perfect condition. When you're looking for your ideal W126, you're as likely to come across cars with sloppy repairs and former accident damage, covered up for sale just as little as necessary, as rust-free, one-owner cars in good shape, which have never needed new paintwork.

When you are looking at the paintwork, concentrate on the formation of blisters on the panel edges and crease lines, and where different panels meet. If you find any, assume that more serious damage may be hidden behind them. Depending on where blisters like this occur, you should consult someone who is familiar with bodywork repairs and can estimate the cost. On the other hand, you can cross off scratches and minor faults under the heading of normal wear and tear, and repair them at your convenience.

The front and rear wheelarches are typically places that harbour rust: they can be quickly checked when viewing the car. Paint scratches can often be dealt with using proprietory scratch repair formulations. If the scratch goes right down to the metal, it will need to be repainted.

Bodywork

4 3 2 1

Look carefully at the entire bodywork and especially the doors, bonnet and boot lid. Remember: no 126-series ever left the factory with uneven panel gaps or dropped doors! They were painstakingly assembled. Bonnets and doors which close poorly or uneven gaps should always make you investigate further. Nearly always, these will have been caused by previous accident damage, which should be used in every case as the basis for a significant reduction in price.

If rust can already be seen along the side panels, the metal underneath will certainly be in much worse state. To be sure, you should remove the plastic moulding.
(Courtesy H-P Lange)

For cars which have been used for many years on motorways or freeways, stone chips will be present around the headlamps and on the bonnet. If not, it's possible that the car has been

Cars did not leave the factory with panel gaps like this. Why has the passenger door been fitted or adjusted too high?

A broken outside mirror is unsightly but can quickly be replaced. A botched repair like this should only be a makeshift solution.

Faded plastics or key scratches around the door handle are cosmetic faults. They can easily be dealt with using the right products such as a deep cleanser for plastics and a colour restorer.

resprayed. In this case too, ask the reason for it. Scratches around the door handles and locks, on the other hand, are quite normal. If the car has been fitted with shiny chrome wheelarch trims, you are right to be suspicious. These were glued in place and dirt and water can collect beneath them. It is not unusual for the wheelarches underneath to be completely rotten.

Underbody

4 3 2 1

If there is a lift or inspection pit available, you should definitely take advantage of it. Have a screwdriver, torch and mirror to hand. Even if everything looks great at first sight, the very thick and tremendously tough PVC underseal applied at the factory can hide a good deal of damage for a long time.

If you notice any inconsistencies in the finish on the underside – they might be small blisters or traces of surface corrosion – press these spots carefully or tap them

Rust on the chrome radiator grille surround is unattractive. If a polishing compound doesn't deal with it, replacing the grille is the only option. Decent secondhand parts are available from about ●x60. (Courtesy C Boucké)

Neglected cars can rust in unusual places, as in this case on the radiator support crossmembers above the headlamps. Welding is difficult here as the metal is very delicate and difficult to shape. (Courtesy C Boucké)

The glue that holds the insulation pad in place under the bonnet dissolves with time, and the pad comes away. It is better to remove it before it comes into contact with moving parts of the engine. (Courtesy C Boucké)

with a screwdriver. In all probability, rust will already have begun its destructive work and you'll feel it crunch. That isn't always a death sentence for the car in question, but there are some key trouble spots, where repairs are very time-consuming and can therefore be expensive.

These include the rear axle mountings. Beware: if these are damaged, the car is no longer safe to drive! Close to these, check the rear jacking points, which can be examined by lifting up the plastic covers in the moulded side panels. Be sure to look at the front jacking points as well.

If the rust has not gone too far, poor jacking points can be refurbished quite well; repair plates are also available. It won't be a cheap job though. Be sure to look under all the wheelarches, especially at the rear, and see whether the banana-shaped wheel liners are still in place. If not, proceed with caution! It's possible that water will already have splashed up for some time behind the side sections and inevitably caused them to rust.

It is essential to examine the underside of the car over an inspection pit or on a lift. The underseal applied by the factory is very tough and can conceal damage for a long time. (Courtesy H-P Lange)

If you don't trust your own judgement of the underbody, make sure to bring an expert with you to view the car. If the car is in bad shape underneath, repairs can quickly outstrip its value. But don't let this section frighten you too much: few cars rust in all these places at the same time, or to the same extent. It is important to know, however, what you might be letting yourself in for.

Weather seals

In general, you should carefully inspect all the seals which you can get to easily. That applies especially to the front and rear screens. If you see milky edges to the glass or

rust bubbling up on the trim strips around the windows, the seal has no longer been doing its job for some time, and a repair will soon be advisable. Making good the rear side window frames on both the saloon and coupé will be particularly expensive. In the engine bay, open all the fluid reservoirs and check the seals on them.

Cooling system

The condition of the radiator can be quickly assessed. When you open the bonnet, it is freely accessible. Is the core in good condition? Are there any traces (usually white) of coolant on its ribs or edges? What colour is the coolant? Has it become very dark? Does it smell of oil or as if something has burnt? Is there enough coolant in the expansion tank?

Lights

Check all the lights work, including the headlamps, rear lights, indicators, brake lights and foglamps. The rear number plate illumination should also work: if it doesn't, it will be considered a defect during an MoT test (in the UK) or similar safety inspection.

Windscreen wipers

Apart from the condition of the wiper blades (are they cracked or hard?), which can quickly be replaced in case of doubt, above all on the 126-series the correct

Are the headlamps clear and free from leaks? Do the reflectors still have their shine? On cars imported from Japan: have the lights been converted to meet local requirements?

The ribbed taillamps are not only striking, but extremely practical. Their design prevents the build-up of too much dirt.

In their resting position, the windscreen wipers should drop back behind the raised rear edge of the bonnet. This is a great advantage in aerodynamic terms.

The small wiper blades for the optional headlamp wash-wipe system are often neglected, although they are very useful.

operation of the wiper mechanism should be checked. When in operation, they run exactly parallel; at rest, they should drop back completely behind the edge of the bonnet.

Windscreen washers

Check the condition and operation of the windscreen washers and headlamp washers. On many cars, the windscreen washers are heated (these can be identified by the heating element inside the washer fluid reservoir). Problems with this are not unknown, but the heating system should work.

Sunroof

Many 126s were delivered from the factory with a sliding roof. Check that this works by opening and closing it several times. Does it operate along its runners quietly, without juddering and reasonably quickly? Does the wind deflector pop up? Does it fold down? Look at the condition of the runners from outside the car with the roof

open. Is the sunroof frame clean, and free from leaves and oily smears? Are the drainage channels clear? These can be checked with a length of wire or an old speedometer cable. Does the headlining around the sunroof show signs of mould, or is it clean? Scrape marks on the paintwork may indicate that the so-called tilt mechanism will soon pack up. Or it may have recently been replaced and not correctly adjusted by the workshop after the repair job.

The sliding roof should be free from leaks, open without difficulty and go all the way back. The tilt mechanism is liable to wear and is sure to need an (expensive) replacement at some stage. Many owners skip the repair and leave the sunroof permanently closed.

Window winders

Check the operation of all the window winders (mechanical and electric). With the good old manual winders, the cable occasionally breaks (particularly on the driver's door); with electric windows, at best it may just be the fuse which is faulty. If a switch is faulty, that is not a serious problem.

Central locking system ④ ③ ② ①

The central locking system is operated by a vacuum system. You can recognise this by the fact that all four doors never actually open and close at exactly the same time, there is always a momentary delay. The main thing is that they open and close! The boot and fuel filler flap are also locked centrally. Check that they work. If an individual door remains shut or opens noticeably slowly, it is usually the result of pressure loss in the system. Often, it is just a hose which is leaking or has come away. It is quite rare for the vacuum pump to be faulty.

Glass: stone chips, milky edges ④ ③ ② ①

First of all, check the windscreen for damage (stone chips and cracks) in the driver's field of vision. These will certainly fail an MoT test or other roadworthiness inspection. You should clarify whether the current owner is prepared to replace the screen or whether you will have to do so. That will be something to negotiate! Milky edges to the front or rear screens indicate leaks in the frame, which you should quickly get to the bottom of. Official testers will still often accept a narrow white band, but it will be noted as a minor fault.

Wheels and tyres ④ ③ ② ①

Check first – especially if the car is fitted with aftermarket wheels – that the wheels have been officially certified for fitment to this model and ask to see the relevant paperwork. For the tyres, check their age (DOT number), tread depth and

On the S-Class, there are no blank switches. You should therefore test all the functions of a well-equipped car like this! (Courtesy Mercedes-Benz AG)

Make sure that the central locking really opens and closes all the doors. If it doesn't, the problem is nearly always due to leaks in the vacuum system. (Courtesy Mercedes-Benz AG)

Left: If the outer edge of the windscreen has turned cloudy and milky, the laminated glass has let in water. When it is replaced, the condition of the frame should also be checked.

Right: It is obvious that this windscreen seal is no longer up to the job. Get rid of it! (Courtesy C Boucké)

wear pattern. If they are
unevenly worn, it may be
necessary to adjust the
alignment. Take a look at
the outer edge of the wheel
rims: is there any kerbing
damage? Incidentally,
original Mercedes-Benz
light alloy wheels were not
stamped with the official
German KBA approval
number.

Wheelarches and liners

Take a torch and shine it
into all four wheelarches.
Are all four liners present?
How do the areas around
the rubber plugs look?
These form a seal for the
inner wheelarches. Traces
of rust are a warning sign!
Are the liners inside the rear
wheelarches present?

With tyres and wheels, pay attention to their age and
originality. It hardly seems believable, but many 126s
were actually delivered new with plain plastic wheel
trims. Their design differed between the first series (top
left) and second series (top right). The optional light
alloy wheels (here the 14-inch version from the first
series, bottom left) received the smooth-faced 15-hole
design only for the second series. Look out for damage,
especially to the rim flange.
(Photo top right courtesy H-P Lange)

Wheel bearings, propshaft and ball joints

If there is any damage to any of these parts, you will discover this during the
test drive, if not before. Faulty wheel bearings, ball joints and propshafts all draw
attention by the noise they make. Screeching or grinding noises, especially when
cornering, give notice that one or more wheel bearings will soon have had it. Ball
joints moan and groan terribly as the front suspension compresses. Repairs are a
matter of routine – parts of different quality levels are very affordable – and needn't
cost a fortune, but the job should not be put off.

Self-levelling rear suspension

Self-levelling suspension was available as an optional extra. As the cars age, faulty
pressure accumulators at the rear of the car are all too common. If the back of
the car stands noticeably high and the rear suspension bounces during the test
drive, then the accumulators are nearly always faulty, and hardly ever the shock
absorbers. Replacements are available from independent parts suppliers and
from brands such as Lemförder (Mercedes' OEM supplier) and Bilstein: they are
inexpensive, as is the job of fitting them by a garage. It will only become pricey if the
garage tries to get you to replace the shock absorbers at the same time. You can
easily spend x1000 doing that, so it is advisable get a second opinion.

Steering

The 126-series cars are fitted with recirculating-ball power steering. This is very light in use, but the steering inherently feels rather indirect. As the cars grow older, the free play in the steering will increase, but should not do so excessively. A professional garage can re-adjust the steering to a certain extent.

Brake callipers and pads 4 3 2 1

When examining the front brakes, turn the front wheels from side to side. You will then have a relatively unobstructed view of the brake callipers and pads. The pads should show a minimum thickness of 2-3mm, which in practice corresponds to the so-called wear limit for driving.

Brake discs (rotors) 4 3 2 1

You will only get a good impression of the brake discs by removing the wheels. When you first examine your chosen car, however, you should at least check through the openings in the wheel whether the disc feels warped or scored. Run your fingertips along the edge of the disc. The more you can feel a clearly raised edge, the more urgent it is to replace the brake disc.

Foot-operated parking brake 4 3 2 1

The parking brake in the footwell often suffers from neglect, especially on cars with automatic transmission. Once the selector is in 'P,' hardly anyone uses it. Later, that can come back to haunt you, when it seizes up and the test inspector finds fault with its inadequate performance. So check how it operates. Can it be released with a clearly audible mechanical sound? How long is the pedal travel? Will it hold the car securely without leaving the car in gear?

The ship-like steering wheel provides limited feedback from the road. If the steering develops any free play as it ages, this impression increases markedly. (Courtesy D Busch)

The poor relation: if you don't use the parking brake in the footwell, you will pay the price when it seizes up.

Under the bonnet (hood) 4 3 2 1

Open the bonnet by pulling on the plastic tongue which pops out when you unlatch the bonnet. Lift up the bonnet and make sure that it can be secured in the vertical service position. Check whether all components are in original condition or if accessory parts from third-party suppliers (performance air filters, etc) have been fitted. How does the engine look to you? Are there noticeable signs of oil or white stains, which might suggest that the coolant has boiled over or leaked out? What state is the accessory drive belt in? Are there any conspicuous noises when the engine is running (clattering or rattling)? Don't be taken in by a freshly cleaned engine! An engine which is getting on in years should look like it's done some work but be free from leaks.

Fuel filler flap and luggage compartment 4 3 2 1

The fuel filler flap is locked and unlocked via the central locking system. Now and again, it can remain locked even though the doors are open. In this case, you will have to actuate it without using the vacuum system (usually by means of a release

An engine bay which genuinely shows its age should look like this: neither too clean nor too dirty, and without any noticeable leaks. (Courtesy H-P Lange)

This isn't regulating anything anymore! The hose line on the retrofitted cold start regulator valve has torn away, so that it is effectively inoperable. Some experts advise against fitting these, as engines with them often exhibit warm-up problems. (Courtesy C Boucké)

device inside the boot – the owner's manual provides further information) and will then be able to open the flap. Take a look to see whether the original sticker with information on the fuel grade and tyre pressures is still there.

What is your impression of the luggage compartment? Is it clean or heavily soiled? Is the (very expensive) carpeting free from damage? Check that the tool kit and first aid kit are complete and in good condition; it's also worth looking at the spare wheel and warning triangle. In addition, keep a lookout for stains from water getting in.

Battery

You will need a multimeter to check the condition of the battery. With the engine idling – and the meter attached to both battery terminals – it should give a reading of between 13.8 and 14.2 volts. With the engine turned off, the reading should be 12.4 to 12.6 volts; if it is lower than 12.4 or even 12 volts, the battery should be replaced.

Water getting in

Check throughout the interior (carpets and seats) for water marks. Feel for signs of dampness inside all the door pockets and lift the carpets in the front footwells. Testing to see if a handkerchief absorbs any moisture will give you a further clue: if it is soaked or just damp, action is required.

Interior
First impression

It is important to form an overall impression. What state are the seats, carpets, trim panels, switches, buttons, steering wheel, gear lever and headlining in? Does it smell musty? Is all the equipment original, or have items such as the steering wheel, seats and audio system been changed by the previous owner(s)? It is so common to find the side bolster on

Press a paper tissue onto the carpet and look underneath the carpeting as well. This will reveal if there is any dampness inside the car.

the driver's seat next to the door worn thin or partly torn that completely undamaged driver's seats on 126s with cloth upholstery are quite exceptional; damage to the bolster should not be used to infer the overall condition of the interior.

Leather (above all on the first series), velour and the rarely ordered 'Amaretta' trim – an alcantara-like material – can withstand many decades of use largely undamaged. Check the adjustment mechanism for the seats (manual and electric), including the lumbar support (inflated using a rather odd hand pump on the first-series cars) and that all the switches and buttons function. Does the interior light come on correctly and switch itself off again?

The condition of the seats will tell you a lot about the previous owner's approach to maintenance. While the brown interior is clearly worn out and discoloured, the blue-grey passenger seat has been very well preserved. Velour upholstery, however, only really shows its age after a very long time. (All photos courtesy H-P Lange)

   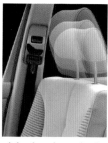

The lavish wood veneer on the centre console can become tarnished and cracked as it ages; it is hard to avoid, especially if the car has been constantly exposed to the sun. The small sunvisor under the interior mirror is very useful on a day-to-day basis. It goes without saying that the adjustable head restraints should move reasonably smoothly. (Courtesy H-P Lange and Mercedes-Benz AG)

Left: Plenty of options in the rear of this car. Right: cracks on the dashboard are common after more than 20 years, especially on cars with blue, red, green or brown trim. (Both photos courtesy H-P Lange)

L-R: The coupé is a four-seater, with two comfortable individual seats in the back.
There is plenty of room to climb into the back without any strain.
An electrically-operated version of the height-adjustable steering wheel was also
available. The well-illuminated vanity mirror is now a sought-after part.
(All photos courtesy Mercedes-Benz AG)

Steering wheel and horn 4 3 2 1

Does the steering wheel appear worn smooth (for wheels with grained plastic rims) or greasy (for leather-covered wheels)? Does the horn work?

Multi-function column stalk 4 3 2 1

Confirm that all the functions of the column stalk, which operates the headlamp main beam, windscreen washer and wipers as well as the indicators, work correctly. Replacements aren't cheap.

Mercedes originally stipulated that the airbags should be replaced every 10-15 years, but later withdrew these instructions. (Courtesy Mercedes-Benz AG)

Instruments 4 3 2 1

The instruments on the W126 are not known for causing problems. Even the optional trip computer – quite a complex device – rarely plays up. You should, however, check that the instrument lighting – and that for the heating and ventilation controls in the centre console – is working, as the bulbs often fail. Replacements are inexpensive – they are simple plug-in bulbs – and fitting them straightforward for experienced home mechanics. Our tip: get the original Mercedes-Benz removal tool for the instrument cluster with a T-handle (part number: 140 589 02 33 00).

Warning lights 4 3 2 1

To determine which warning lights are fitted to each car, you have to know exactly what equipment it has. You can read in the owner's manual what the different warning lights signify. When you turn on the ignition without starting the engine, all the lights should come on. On the diesel models, which are exceedingly rare in Europe, check the glow plug warning light on the far right, which should go out after a few seconds.

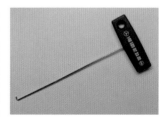

Mercedes' original extractor tool to remove the instrument cluster is a valuable aid ... and not expensive.

One quirk of the W126 is that the ABS warning light coming on doesn't always indicate a fault in the system. Sometimes it's just that the voltage is too low. Hold on and switch the engine off and on again. If the ABS light goes out after a few moments, the anti-block braking system is okay. If you have any doubts, it is better of course to have the fault examined.

As they become older, many of the warning lights will no longer glow as brightly, but they should still all work. The trip computer (to the right) is a feature much appreciated by enthusiasts. (Courtesy Mercedes-Benz AG)

Suspension [4] [3] [2] [1]

The suspension is considered pretty tough. Caution is advised if a car has been modified, for example if the suspension has been lowered or extremely wide tyres fitted. If you are considering such a car, you should get the suspension checked over in a garage.

Exhaust system [4] [3] [2] [1]

You will be able to see and hear leaks in the exhaust system. If that does prove the case, you needn't worry too much, even high-quality replacements are affordable. Renewing the entire exhaust system on a V8, especially the 5.6-litre model, on the other hand, is a major investment. If modifications (such as fitting a performance exhaust) have been made, you should make sure that the changes have been approved and correctly carried out. Ask to see the paperwork.

Check whether the standard exhaust system is fitted. If not, is any necessary certification paperwork available?

Oil leaks [4] [3] [2] [1]

It is easiest to check if a car is free from oil leaks after a test drive. Park the car on level ground and place some cardboard under the engine. No oil should drip onto it. If it does, take a close look at the engine.

Coolant leaks [4] [3] [2] [1]

See if any coolant is seeping out under the front of the car. Light-coloured marks on the external components of the cooling system (hoses and clamps) may indicate leaks.

Fluids [4] [3] [2] [1]

Check the age and condition of all fluids, ideally referring to any maintenance documents and service tags in the engine compartment. If any of them – with the exception of the engine oil – are noticeably dark, they should definitely be changed. 'Black' coolant or brake fluid is definitely not normal!

Transmission leaks [4] [3] [2] [1]

The gearbox and differential can also develop leaks. After your test drive, look for fresh traces of oil.

Left: take in different types of road surface during the test drive. Listen out for noises from the suspension. Right: you don't have to go to these extremes! You can also test whether the car will stay in its lane under normal conditions.

Test drive

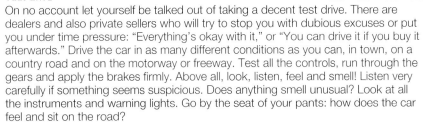

On no account let yourself be talked out of taking a decent test drive. There are dealers and also private sellers who will try to stop you with dubious excuses or put you under time pressure: "Everything's okay with it," or "You can drive it if you buy it afterwards." Drive the car in as many different conditions as you can, in town, on a country road and on the motorway or freeway. Test all the controls, run through the gears and apply the brakes firmly. Above all, look, listen, feel and smell! Listen very carefully if something seems suspicious. Does anything smell unusual? Look at all the instruments and warning lights. Go by the seat of your pants: how does the car feel and sit on the road?

Making really sure

A former owner who is confident in his car will certainly have no objection if you want to have the car checked over by an independent inspector. Many garages, car clubs and vehicle testing organisations offer used car inspections. Naturally, these aren't free of charge, and the seller is unlikely to accept these costs. You should therefore feel pretty certain that the model you are looking at really is your next car. But the bottom line is that a professional assessment like this is a win for both parties.

Evaluation procedure

Now add up the points from each section.
152 points = An outstanding car, which is sure to increase in value.
115-151 points = Good to very good, you can buy this car without hesitation.
77-114 points = Average to good, but what problems have you found?
39-76 points = Below average to fair. Think carefully about the purchase.
38 or fewer points = You will need to invest some money in the car. If the price is particularly attractive and you have some mechanical skills, it may be worth a bet, but only then. The complete restoration of a W126 is not (yet) worthwhile, there are enough good cars out there.

10 Auctions
– sold! Another way to buy your dream

Auction pros & cons

Pros: Prices are often lower than those of dealers or private sellers and you might grab a real bargain on the day. Auctioneers have generally established clear title with the seller. At the venue you can usually examine documentation relating to the vehicle.

Cons: You have to rely on a sketchy catalogue description of condition and history. The opportunity to inspect is limited and you cannot drive the car. Auction cars are often a little below par and may require some work. It's easy to overbid. There will usually be a buyer's premium to pay in addition to the auction hammer price.

Which auction?

Auctions by established auctioneers are advertised in car magazines and on the auction houses' websites. A catalogue, or a simple printed list of the lots for auctions might only be available a day or two ahead, though often lots are listed and pictured on auctioneers' websites much earlier. Contact the auction company to ask if previous auction selling prices are available, as this is useful information (details of past sales are often available on websites).

Catalogue, entry fee, and payment details

When you purchase the catalogue of vehicles in an auction, it often acts as a ticket allowing two people to attend the viewing days and the auction. Catalogue details tend to be comparatively brief, but will include information such as 'one owner from new, low mileage, full service history,' etc. It will also usually show a guide price to give you some idea of what to expect to pay and will tell you what is charged as a 'Buyer's premium.' The catalogue will also contain details of acceptable forms of payment. At the fall of the hammer an immediate deposit is usually required, the balance payable within 24 hours. If the plan is to pay by cash, there may be a cash limit. Some auctions will accept payment by debit card. Sometimes credit or charge cards are acceptable but will often incur an extra charge. A bank draft or bank transfer will have to be arranged in advance with your own bank as well as with the auction house. No car will be released before all payments are cleared. If delays occur in payment transfers, then storage costs can accrue.

Buyer's premium

A buyer's premium will be added to the hammer price: don't forget this in your calculations. It is not usual for there to be a further state tax or local tax on the purchase price and/or on the buyer's premium.

Viewing

In some instances, it's possible to view on the day, or days before, as well as in the hours prior to, the auction. There are auction officials available who are willing to help out by opening engine and luggage compartments and to allow you to inspect the interior. While the officials may start the engine for you, a test drive is out of the question. Crawling under and around the car as much as you want is permitted, but you can't suggest that the car you are interested in be jacked up or attempt to do the job yourself. You can also ask to see any documentation available.

Bidding

Before you take part in the auction, decide your maximum bid – and stick to it! It may take a while for the auctioneer to reach the lot you are interested in, so use that time to observe how other bidders behave. When it's the turn of your car, attract the auctioneer's attention and make an early bid. The auctioneer will then look to you for a reaction every time another bid is made, usually the bids will be in fixed increments until the bidding slows, when smaller increments will often be accepted before the hammer falls. If you want to withdraw from the bidding, make sure the auctioneer understands your intentions – a vigorous shake of the head when he or she looks to you for the next bid should do the trick! Assuming that you are the successful bidder, the auctioneer will note your card or paddle number, and from that moment on you will be responsible for the vehicle. If the car is unsold, either because it failed to reach the reserve or because there was little interest, it may be possible to negotiate with the owner, via the auctioneers, after the sale is over.

Successful bid

There are two more items to think about. How to get the car home, and insurance. If you can't drive the car, your own or a hired trailer is one way, another is to have the vehicle shipped using the facilities of a local company. The auction house will also have details of companies specialising in the transfer of cars.

Insurance for immediate cover can usually be purchased on site, but it may be more cost-effective to make arrangements with your own insurance company in advance, and then call to confirm the full details.

eBay and other online auctions

eBay and other online auctions could land you a car at a bargain price, though you'd be foolhardy to bid without examining the car first, something most vendors encourage. A useful feature of eBay is that the geographical location of the car is shown, so you can narrow your choices to those within a realistic radius of home. Be prepared to be outbid in the last few moments of the auction. Remember, your bid is binding and that it will be very, very difficult to get restitution in the case of a crooked vendor fleecing you – caveat emptor!

Be aware that some cars offered for sale in online auctions are 'ghost' cars. Don't part with any cash without being sure that the vehicle actually exists and is as described (usually pre-bidding inspection is possible).

Auctioneers

Barrett-Jackson www.barrett-jackson.com/ **Bonhams** www.bonhams.com/ **British Car Auctions (BCA)** www.bca.com/ **Coys** www.coys.co.uk/ **eBay** www.eBay.com/ **Gooding & Company** www.goodingco.com/ **H&H** www.handh.co.uk/ **Mecum** www.mecum.com/ **RM Sotheby's** https://rmsothebys.com/ **Shannons** www.shannons.com.au/ **Silver** www.silverauctions.com

11 Paperwork

– correct documentation is essential!

The paper trail

Enthusiasts' cars often come with a large portfolio of paperwork accumulated by a succession of proud owners. This documentation represents the real history of the car and shows the level of care the car has received, how it's been used, which specialists have worked on it and the dates of major repairs.

Registration documents

All countries/states have some form of registration for private vehicles, whether it's like the American 'pink slip' system or the British 'log book' system.

It is essential to check that the registration document is genuine, that it relates to the car in question, and that all the vehicle's details are correctly recorded, including chassis/VIN and engine numbers (if these are shown). If you are buying from the previous owner, his or her name and address will be recorded in the document; but not if you are buying from a dealer. In the UK, the current registration document is named 'V5C,' and is printed in coloured sections of blue, green and pink. The blue section relates to the car specification, the green section has details of the new owner and the pink section is sent to the DVLA in the UK when the car is sold. A small section in yellow deals with selling the car within the motor trade. If the car has a foreign registration, there may be expensive and time-consuming formalities to complete. Do you really want the hassle?

Roadworthiness certificate

Most country/state administrations require that vehicles are regularly tested to prove that they are safe to use on public roads and do not produce excessive emissions. In the UK the MoT test is carried out at approved testing stations, for a fee. In the US the requirement varies, but most states insist on an emissions test every two years as a minimum, while the police are charged with pulling over unsafe-looking vehicles.

In the UK, the test is required on an annual basis once a vehicle becomes three years old. Of particular relevance for older cars is that the certificate issued includes the mileage reading recorded at the test date and, therefore, becomes an independent record of that car's history. Ask the seller if previous certificates are available. Without an MoT the vehicle should be trailered to its new home, unless you insist that a valid MoT is part of the deal. (Not such a bad idea this, as at least you will know the car was roadworthy on the day it was tested and you don't need to wait for the old certificate to expire before having the test done.)

Road licence

The administration of nearly every country/state charges some kind of tax for the use of its road system, the actual form of the 'road licence,' and how it is displayed, varying enormously country to country and state to state.

Whatever the form of the 'road licence,' it must relate to the vehicle carrying it and must be present and valid if the car is to be driven on the public highway legally. Current legislation in the UK means that the seller of a car must surrender any existing road fund licence, and it is the responsibility of the new owner to re-tax the vehicle at the time of purchase and before the car can be driven on the road. It's therefore vital to see the Vehicle Registration Certificate (V5C) at the time of purchase, and to have access to the New Keeper Supplement (V5C/2), allowing the buyer to obtain road tax immediately.

If the car is untaxed because it has not been used for a period of time, the owner has to inform the licensing authorities, otherwise the vehicle's date-related registration number will be lost and there will be a painful amount of paperwork to get it re-registered.

Valuation certificate

A private vendor may have a recent valuation certificate, or letter signed by a recognised expert stating how much he, or she, believes the particular car to be worth (such documents, together with photos, are usually needed to get 'agreed value' insurance). Generally, such documents should act only as confirmation of your own assessment of the car rather than a guarantee of value. The easiest way to find out how to obtain a formal valuation is to contact the owners' club.

Data cards and VIN

Each Mercedes left the factory with a detailed data card, specifying the exact model, colour and trim, and the codes for each option fitted. These codes – which you can look up on many online sites – should correspond to the actual equipment on the car you are viewing and provide valuable confirmation of its authenticity. If the card is missing, Mercedes-Benz' Classic department or dealer in your country may be able to supply a replacement. These codes are repeated on the stamped metal plate on the bonnet slam panel.

The 17-digit VIN (Vehicle Identification Number) on the data card should tally with that on the car, which you can find on a plate on the bonnet slam panel and stamped on the bulkhead.

Service history

Try to obtain as much service history and other paperwork pertaining to the car as you can. Naturally, dealer stamps, or specialist garage receipts score most points in the value stakes. However, anything helps in the great authenticity game, items like the original bill of sale, handbook, parts invoices and repair bills adding to the story and the character of the car. Even a brochure correct to the year of the car's manufacture is a useful document and something that you could well have to search hard to locate in future years. If the seller claims that the car has been restored, then expect receipts and other evidence from a specialist restorer.

If the seller claims to have carried out regular servicing at home, ask what work was completed and when, and to seek some evidence of it being carried out. Your assessment of the car's overall condition should tell you whether the seller's claims are genuine.

Restoration photographs

If the seller tells you that the car has undergone significant work, ask to be shown a series of photographs taken while the work was under way. These should help you gauge the thoroughness of the work. If you buy the car, ask if you can have the photographs, as they form an important part of the vehicle's history. It's surprising how many sellers are happy to part with their car but want to hang on to their photographs! You may, however, be able to persuade the vendor to get a set of copies made.

12 What's it worth?
– let your head rule your heart

The 126-series has long been considered a classic, and many enthusiasts regard it as the most attractive S-Class of all. Cars from the first series (until 1985) can already be registered as historic vehicles in many countries, provided they are in original condition. Large numbers of second-series cars with standard emissions control equipment still take on the rough and tumble of everyday traffic quite unfazed.

It is only logical that estimated prices for cars which dropped out of used car price guides a long time ago vary greatly on an individual basis. This leaves a good deal of latitude, for dealers as well as private sellers. You can cash in on the 'Classic' label.

It's a fact: good, well maintained cars with a documented service history and no maintenance work outstanding are not getting any cheaper. Instead, their market value is slowly but surely increasing. A price estimate of around ●x18,000 for a 560 SEL in top condition can therefore be completely justified. You can still pick up a decent 300 SE, however, for less than half that much.

If you can't invest at least ●x6-7000 – and have some cash spare for potential work on the car – you would do better not to take a gamble on the S-Class. Even if drivable cars are offered for sale from ●x3000, the follow-up costs on a supposed bargain like this can assume horrifying proportions. Nonetheless, offers like this keep on appearing. What matters when you're looking for a new set of wheels is to keep a cool head and not let your heart or gut feeling take the decision for you. Even if the supposed car of your dreams is parked in front of you!

This family look characterised an entire generation of Mercedes. (Courtesy Mercedes-Benz AG)

Its flowing lines ensure that an S-Class which is now more than 30 years old still comes across as truly timeless. (Courtesy Mercedes-Benz AG)

Today no one would dare order a luxury car in red, even though the colour suits the big saloon very well. (Courtesy Mercedes-Benz AG)

There is no such thing as a fully-equipped car

Many sellers base their exaggerated asking price on the notion that the car in question is a rare 'fully loaded' model. In truth, no such car exists! Even at a time when Mercedes had yet to develop its equipment lines and packages, and new car buyers could choose the individual specification of their cars, it was never possible

A second control panel for the radio in the rear centre armrest was, like many other features, available as an option at extra cost. (Courtesy MBIG eV)

to combine all the available options shown in the brochure in a single car. Some options were not offered with all engines or fitted to all body styles. If a seller spins you the 'fully equipped' story (which unfortunately happens nearly all the time in the world of classic Mercedes), you can quietly smile and ignore it.

Condition

Just one thing matters: what is standing in front of you? With the help of the rating system in Chapter 9, you can now assess the condition of the car on offer and whether it is worthwhile to start negotiating with the seller. In addition, it makes sense to find out about the current market situation beforehand (eg through the relevant websites) and to look at specialist magazines such as *Mercedes Enthusiast* or *Classic Mercedes* (see Chapter 16, The Community). In the case of Mercedes-Benz, it is always worthwhile getting in touch with the lively enthusiast community. Clubs will often be very helpful, even to non-members. As a rule, you can get a pretty good idea of the going price from sources like these.

Obviously, you can pay correspondingly more for a really well-cared for car with one retired owner, which has been kept in a garage. And such cars really do exist! But you should be aware that the asking price will depend not only on the condition per se, but on the extras which are fitted.

An airbag is always a strong selling point. (Courtesy Mercedes-Benz AG)

Desirable options/extras
Automatic transmission
Sliding roof
Velour or leather upholstery (leather on the first series of higher quality)

Left: Many enthusiasts prefer the hard-wearing velour trim to leather.
Centre: The classic 15-hole alloy wheels look good on any W126 and are therefore also popular secondhand. (Courtesy H-P Lange)
Right: Some S-Class fans will change the entire instrument cluster to get hold of the trip computer. (Courtesy Mercedes-Benz AG)

Orthopaedic driver's seat
Original radio (Becker)
Metallic paint
Original alloy wheels
Air conditioning (the manual 'Heizmatic' system is preferable to the automatic climate control)
Catalytic converter (petrol engines)

Undesirable features
Unapproved or non-standard accessories (tuning)
Tow hitch
Non-standard paint colours
'Poverty spec' cars, without any extras

Exceptions
The so-called 'wrong' colours are those finishes which were admittedly available from the factory, but which were rarely ordered. The iridescent turquoise 'Beryl' metallic (colour code 888), the actually not uncommon 'Almandine Red (512) or the special finish Mimosa Yellow (618) – which seems quite bizarre today – are generally colours which justify a price reduction, as they are reputedly hard to sell. Recently though, a group of collectors has begun to emerge in the W126 community who are specifically looking for such cars, preferably with interior trim in an unusual colour as well. Basic cars – the so-called 'poverty spec' models – which are inherently unpopular, are becoming more and more attractive to enthusiasts, who take as their motto: "If it isn't there, it can't go wrong."

Warranties
The matter of warranties on older cars is always difficult. Even when you buy from a dealer, who is obliged to offer a warranty, there are always times when some traders try to get out of it. There can be sales agreements with dubious disclaimers, which release the trader from any liability and transfer all the risk to the buyer. In such cases it may often be said that the car is really only intended for export. If talk like

Mimosa Yellow (618) was a special paint finish, which must have been very rarely ordered. In combination with the Olive leather interior trim, this 500 SE is in all likelihood unique. It is certainly an eye-catcher. (Both photos courtesy D Busch)

The combination of Signal Red (568) paintwork with protective side mouldings in Mussel Grey (176) and a red leather interior is exceedingly stylish. For a modern car it might seem out-of-place and disconcerting, but the 126 saloon wears it with dignity. (Both photos courtesy S Mantel)

that makes you feel uneasy, back away from the deal and look around for a more reputable dealer. Mind you, when you buy from a private seller, you always take the risk yourself!

Pre-purchase inspection
To keep the risk to a minimum, first, you have this book in your hand, and secondly, you can call on the help of independent experts. A seller who has nothing to hide should agree to a technical inspection of the car you are considering buying in a garage (it doesn't have to be a Mercedes dealership) or by a vehicle testing organisation. You will have to bear the cost of this, which is normally worthwhile. If the seller is sceptical, you can argue that he or she will be better able to evaluate their car after a professional inspection. It's really a win-win for everyone.

Striking a deal
Most importantly, insist on a written sales agreement! Striking a deal on a handshake has its charm, but definitely not between two strangers. Negotiate the price on the basis of the actual condition of the car, its mileage, the service documentation available, and any faults. Take into account the specification and body style: coupés are worth more than saloons. If you can see that immediate repairs or service work will be required, deduct the cost of these from the purchase price, or negotiate with the seller to put right some of these faults before the sale. Always be fair! Part of every negotiation is to meet each other in the middle, and to agree a price which both parties can live with. If that just isn't possible, keep looking! There are so many well maintained 126s on the market that you will always find a decent car somewhere.

13 Do you really want to restore?

– it'll take longer and cost more than you think

There is a good reason why many 126s which have been taken off the road in Europe are exported to Africa: at heart, the W126 is a strongly built car which uses straightforward technology that is well laid out for ease of maintenance. Of course, depending on the equipment fitted to it, an S-Class has its measure of electronic components: these should not be underestimated and require specialist knowledge and the right equipment to service and repair them. Mechanically speaking, however, any skilled mechanic will basically find a way to keep the car running. As one master mechanic from Morocco put it: "With the gift for improvisation of young people in my country, an old Merc like this will run forever."

Despite its very sturdy body construction – even by today's standards – stripping down, repairing and reassembling the 126-series is not an insurmountable challenge if you have some experience, especially as there are enough replacement parts (new and used) available. There is no need to fall back on reproduction parts; most items are still available from the parts department of your Mercedes dealership.

It is possible to save money with secondhand parts from dealers or scrap yards, and the internet can also be a useful resource.

This SEC is only used for parts. Given the range of cars on offer, a restoration is currently uneconomic. (Courtesy MBIG eV)

Be wary of cars which already have visible repairs or were patched up cheaply to get through a safety inspection. You will always pay a price for sloppy work!

As far as electrical and electronic components such as ECUs are concerned, there is a good selection of used parts available across the price range, with some suppliers offering components that have been tested with a guarantee. You can't check the operation of an ABS control unit on the kitchen table, so you should only buy from suppliers you can trust!

Questions and answers

Is it worthwhile restoring a car like the Mercedes 126-series which is still on the road in such large numbers? Not really. First, there are still enough good cars that, in case of doubt, it pays to keep on looking rather than waste a lot of money on a down-at-heel car.

Secondly, the W126 – with the exception of a few very well maintained coupés and rare AMG versions – does not yet command such elevated prices to justify a costly restoration to maintain or increase the value of the car. That will certainly change in the foreseeable future.

For the moment, in most cases the comprehensive restoration of a W126 –

especially if it is carried out by a professional workshop – will end up costing so much that it will amount to a total loss in economic terms. Unless the car in question is an extremely rare version or you have a personal connection to it ("It was Grandad's Merc, I absolutely have to keep it!"), you should avoid a complete restoration on financial grounds.

With a model still as common as the W126 saloon, you should ask yourself whether you really want to take on a restoration. Of course, improving an already decent car is always worthwhile. (Courtesy H-P Lange)

There is no question: this car has been well looked after and not restored. Some preventive maintenance jobs can prove costly, but a well-maintained coupé will hardly ever go down in value. (Courtesy H-P Lange)

14 Paint problems
– bad complexion, including dimples, pimples and bubbles

Paint faults generally occur due to lack of protection/maintenance, or to poor preparation prior to a respray or touch-up. Measuring the paint depth on each panel will help confirm if all the paint is original. Some of the following conditions may be present in the car you're looking at:

Orange peel
This appears as an uneven paint surface, similar to the skin of an orange. This fault is caused by the failure of atomised paint droplets to flow into each other when they hit the surface. It's sometimes possible to rub out the effect with proprietary paint cutting/rubbing compound or very fine grades of abrasive paper. A respray may be necessary in severe cases. Consult a bodywork repairer/paint shop for advice on the particular car.

Cracking
Severe cases are likely to have been caused by too heavy an application of paint (or filler beneath the paint). Also, insufficient stirring of the paint before application can lead to the components being improperly mixed, and cracking can result. Incompatibility with the paint already on the panel can have a similar effect. To rectify the problem, it is necessary to rub down to a smooth, sound finish before respraying the problem area.

Crazing
Sometimes the paint takes on a crazed rather than a cracked appearance when the problems mentioned under 'Cracking' are present. This problem can also be caused by a reaction between the underlying surface and the paint. Paint removal and respraying the problem area is usually the only solution.

Blistering
Almost always caused by corrosion of the metal beneath the paint. Usually perforation will be found in the metal and

the damage will usually be worse than that suggested by the area of blistering. The metal will have to be repaired before repainting.

Micro blistering
Usually the result of an economy respray where inadequate heating has allowed moisture to settle on the car before spraying. Consult a paint specialist, but usually damaged paint will have to be removed before partial or full respraying. Can also be caused by car covers that don't 'breathe.'

Fading
Some colours, especially reds, are prone to fading if subjected to strong sunlight for long periods without the benefit of polish protection. Sometimes proprietary paint restorers and/or paint cutting/rubbing compounds will retrieve the situation. Often a respray is the only real solution.

Peeling
Often a problem with metallic paintwork when the sealing lacquer becomes damaged and begins to peel off. Poorly applied paint may also peel. The remedy is to strip and start again!

Dimples
Dimples in the paintwork are caused by the residue of polish (particularly silicone types) not being removed properly before respraying. Paint removal and repainting is the only solution.

15 Problems due to lack of use
– just like their owners, W126s need exercise!

The best Mercedes is one which is regularly driven and maintained. However tempting the car with one retired owner which has been kept in a garage and polished with a handkerchief, and which has covered a certified 40,000 miles, it may not be the best on offer! Later, when you want to use a car like this on a regular basis, its condition may suffer from this period of immobilisation, resulting in costly repairs. Among club members, cars with 150,000 miles and an up-to-date service history are clearly favoured. Cars are for driving! If you only use a W126 for high days and holidays, you can of course consider a low-mileage car.

This characteristic corrosion on the edge of the boot lid is still harmless but should be dealt with promptly. (Courtesy H-P Lange)

Corrosion

Cars which have seen little of the road in their lives rarely suffer from body corrosion. For the most part, they spend their days and nights in dry garages. Instead, rust gnaws away unseen, preferring mechanical components like the braking system, where the pistons, callipers and cylinders can be affected, or where the brake pads can be seized onto the discs (rotors). Rust can also cause the parking brake mechanism to seize, to the point where it is sometimes impossible to move the car at all. It is not uncommon for the flywheel to stick to the clutch plate. It is better not to move a car like this until the problem has been fixed.

Fluids

Fluids which are too old should be replenished before you drive a car which has been standing for a long time. Old oil can attack seals and gaskets, and damage bearings. Some constituents of fuel and brake fluid can absorb water from the air over time, which can lead to corrosion in the fuel lines and braking system. If the brake fluid has already absorbed too much water, vapour bubbles can form in the system when the brakes are hot. In the worst case, the brakes may fail!

In the engine bay, look out for oil and coolant leaks. If the car has self-levelling suspension, check the additional fluid reservoir. (Courtesy Mercedes-Benz AG)

Tyres

It is a common misconception that tyres whose profile still looks quite alright can be used without any worries. After just five to seven years, the softening agents in the tyre compound can lose their effectiveness, and the tyre will become brittle and cracked. That can put your life at risk!

When you are buying a car, look at the DOT number moulded into the tyre

wall. This gives the year and week of production. If the car has been standing for a long time, flat spots may have developed. These can be felt clearly as vibrations when driving, although they can disappear again. If they don't, you should have the tyres checked by a professional and, if necessary, replaced.

Shock absorbers

As a rule, shock absorbers rarely suffer from periods of immobilisation. You may have the opportunity to look underneath with the car on a lift. If the shock absorbers are suspiciously damp, fluid may already be seeping out. In this case, the seals inside the shock absorbers may be leaking. This is caused by the seals ageing and becoming brittle. Shock absorbers like this should be replaced immediately. The good old 'bounce test' (pressing down hard on all four corners of the car) is at best only an indication of the condition of the suspension and not a reliable diagnosis. If the car bounces noticeably as it rebounds, it requires attention. Take particular care if you are looking at a car that has been fitted with sports suspension. Sometimes this is so firm that it won't bounce anyway. In general, a car like this should be examined by a specialist. The optional hydropneumatic suspension on the W126 guarantees excellent roadholding … provided it is in good order and free from leaks. These should, however, be expected as the car becomes older. Repairs can be very expensive. To avoid the risk, you may prefer to stick to the conventional suspension, which the engineers set up very well at the time for this heavy car.

Rubber and plastic parts

After more than 20 years, the softening agents in all kinds of rubber seals can lose their effectiveness, and the seals will have hardened. Even regular care with the appropriate sprays or roll-on pens will only delay this process. In the worst case, the window seals, for example, will shrink so much that water can run into the doors from above. A thorough check of all the seals concerned (doors, windows, sunroof

etc) should go without saying.

Faded bumpers, protection strips and mirror casings are more cosmetic in nature. Over time unpainted plastic parts become grey and unsightly. You can deal with these problems effectively using the right care products. If you are unsure about doing it yourself, turn to a professional car detailer. It is often hard to believe what experts can do with cars that are obviously tired, even when it comes to their paintwork. And in many places, it is cheaper than you'd think.

As the number of features increases, so too does the potential for trouble. Convenience features can stop working. Owners of 'poverty spec' models definitely have the advantage here. (Courtesy H-P Lange)

Electrics

The biggest enemy of correctly functioning electrical systems is oxidation. It can affect plug connectors and contacts, often leading to malfunctions or the outright failure of complete modules. If a car has been standing for a long time, you should therefore thoroughly test all the important functions. If you do find a defect, there is no need to bring out your complete tool kit straight away. In many cases, spraying the contacts or using some fine sandpaper on the connectors can work wonders. Even fuses pack up but can be replaced in no time. Normally, it will do your car good to connect the battery to a trickle charger (also known as a 'Battery Tender') if you expect it to be immobilised for a longer time. This simulates the charging and discharging process in daily use and so keeps the battery fresh.

Exhaust system

It is almost a law of nature, and not just for the Mercedes W126: when you buy a car that hasn't moved for months, after a few weeks' use the exhaust system will give up the ghost. Even if it still looks undamaged, the water contained in the emissions will let rust develop in the silencer and tailpipe. It is almost inevitable that they will rust from the inside out. Unless, that is, the car has been fitted with a stainless steel exhaust system, but even that is no guarantee against corrosion.

Exhaust systems usually rust from the inside out. If the car has been standing for a long time, the exhaust may fail after it has been driven for a short while, even though it appears undamaged from the outside. (Courtesy H-P Lange)

16 The Community

— key people, organisations and companies in the W126 world

Clubs

Mercedes-Benz lends its support to more than 80 independent clubs worldwide, and many of these have model registers dedicated to the W126. Benefits available to members include technical helplines and other information, discounted services such as insurance, professionally produced club magazines and the chance to join frequent social and driving events. You can find out more at:

• Mercedes-Benz Classic (factory homepage): www.mercedes-benz.com/en/ mercedes-benz/classic/classic-overview/
• UK: www.mercedes-benz-club.co.uk/
• North America: www.mbca.org
• Other countries: specials.mercedes-benz-classic.com/en/club/#ger

Specialists

In North America, it's worth starting with one of the 85 local sections of the club, which should be able to recommend a dealer or workshop near you.

In the UK, one company has made the W126 its speciality: the SEC Shop, in Kent (www.sec-shop.coms). Despite its name, it caters to both the saloon and coupé models.

Many other independent Mercedes specialists such as those listed below often sell good-quality examples of the W126 and can arrange servicing and other repair work on them:

A pair of face-lifted S-Class saloons. (Courtesy Mercedes-Benz Classic)

- Edward Hall (Buckinghamshire): www.edward-hall.co.uk/
- John Haynes Mercedes (West Sussex): http://www.john-haynes.com/
- Charles Ironside (Hampshire): http://www.charlesironside.co.uk/

You will find listings for many other companies in the club directories and in the magazines below.

Parts and accessories

Many service parts remain available from your local Mercedes-Benz dealer, with support from the factory in Germany or the Mercedes-Benz Classic Center in Irvine, California. Their prices can sometimes be high, so you may prefer to order online from an independent parts supplier such as these:

- UK – Mercedes Parts Centre: www.mercedes-parts-centre.co.uk/ and PFS Parts: www.partsformercedes-benz.com/
- US – Pelican Parts: www.pelicanparts.com/Mercedes-Benz/index-SC.htm

Useful sources of information

Three English-language magazines cater to classic Mercedes enthusiasts and often feature the W126:

- *Mercedes Enthusiast* (monthly – www.mercedesenthusiast.co.uk/) and *Classic Mercedes* (quarterly – www.classicmercedesmagazine.com/) can be found at large newsstands in both the UK and North America, or obtained on subscription.
- *Mercedes-Benz Classic* is published in English and German by Mercedes itself three times a year: subscribe at www.mercedes-benz.com/en/mercedes-benz/lifestyle/classic-magazine/

Nik Greene's recent book, *Buying and Maintaining a 126 S-Class Mercedes* (Crowood, 2017), is dedicated to the W126, while James Taylor's earlier book, *Mercedes-Benz S-Class 1972-2013* (Crowood, 2013), sets the W126 in its historical context. Brooklands Books (www.brooklandsbooks.co.uk) devotes one of its excellent compilations of period road tests to the W126: *Mercedes S-Class 1980-1991 Limited Edition Extra*.

For enthusiasts who want to carry out repair work themselves, Kent Bergsma's informative Mercedes source website (https://mercedessource.com) and associated YouTube channel have a wealth of 'How To' information for the W126. In the UK, the official club (https://mercedes-benz-club.co.uk/) has an active model-specific forum covering common problems and how to fix them. Even if you do not plan on doing the work yourself, these resources provide valuable guidance on how difficult (and potentially expensive) a repair may be.

17 Vital statistics
– essential data at your fingertips

All models

Drive type	Rear-wheel drive
Body construction	All-steel body, unitary construction
Front suspension	Independent, with dual wishbones, coil springs and anti-roll bar	**Rear suspension**	Semi-trailing arms with coil springs and anti-roll bar
Steering	Recirculating-ball, with power assistance

Series 1 models

Model	280 S	280 SE/SEL**	380 SE/SEL**/SEC*	500 SE/SEL**/SEC*
Years built	1979-1985	1979-1985	1979-85 (* from 1981)	1979-85 (* from 1981)
Body style	Four-door saloon	Four-door saloon	Four-door saloon/ two-door coupé	Four-door saloon/ two-door coupé
Engine	In-line six-cylinder (carburettor) M 110	In-line six-cylinder (fuel injection) M 110	V8 (fuel injection) M 116	V8 (fuel injection) M 117
Capacity (cc)	2746	2746	3818/3839 (from 1981)	4973
Power output (bhp)	154	182	215/201 (from 1981)	237/228 (from 1981)
Mixture	Twin-choke downdraught carburettor	Bosch K-Jetronic fuel injection	Bosch K-Jetronic fuel injection	Bosch K-Jetronic fuel injection
Transmission	4M/5M or 4A	4M/5M or 4A	4A	4A
Tyres	195/70 or 205/70 HR 14	195/70 or 205/70 HR 14	205/70 VR 14	205/70 VR 14
Dimensions: mm (in)				
Length	4995 (196.6)	4995/5135** (196.6/202.2)	4995 (196.6)/ 5135 (202.2)**/ 4910 (193.3)*	4995 (196.6)/ 5135 (202.2)**/ 4910 (193.3)*
Width	1820 (71.7)	1820 (71.7)	1820 (71.7)/1828 (72.0)*	1820 (71.7)/ 1828 (72.0)*
Height	1430 (56.3)	1430 (56.3)/ 1434 (56.5)	1436 (56.5)/1440 (56.7)**/1407 (55.4)*	1436 (56.5)/ 1440 (56.7)**/ 1407 (55.4)*
Unladen weight: kg (lb)	1610 (3549)	1610 (3549)/ 1640 (3616)**	1645 (3627)/ 1665 (3671)**/ 1585 (3494)*	1670 (3682)/ 1705 (3759)**/ 1650 (3638)*
Units built	42,996	133,955/20,655**	58,239/27,014**/ 11,267*	21,748/56,770**/ 23,373*

Series 2 models

Model	260 SE	300 SE/SEL**	420 SE/SEL**/ SEC*	500 SE/SEL**/ SEC*	560 SE/SEL**/ SEC*
Years built	1985-91	1985-91	1985-91	1985-91	1985-91
Body style	Four-door saloon	Four-door saloon	Four-door saloon/two-door coupé	Four-door saloon/two-door coupé	Four-door saloon/two-door coupé
Engine	In-line six-cylinder (fuel injection) M 103	In-line six-cylinder (fuel injection) M 103	V8 (fuel injection) M 116	V8 (fuel injection) M 117	V8 (fuel injection) M 117
Capacity (cc)	2597	2962	4196	4973	5547
Power output (bhp)	164 (Cat: 158)	185 (Cat: 177)	215 (Cat: 198)/228 (Cat: 221) from 1987	242 (Cat: 220)/261 (Cat: 249) from 1987	296 (ECE-spec) or 268/Cat: 239 or 275
Mixture	Bosch KE-Jetronic fuel injection	Bosch KE-Jetronic fuel injection	Bosch KE-Jetronic fuel injection	Bosch KE-Jetronic fuel injection	Bosch KE-Jetronic fuel injection
Transmission	5M or 4A	5M or 4A	4A	4A	4A
Tyres	205/65 VR 15	205/65 VR 15	205/65 VR 15	205/65 VR 15	215/65 VR 15
Dimensions - mm (in):					
Length	5020 (197.6)	5020 (197.6)/ 5160 (203.1)**	5020 (197.6)/ 5160 (203.1)**/ 4935 (194.3)*	5020 (197.6)/ 5160 (203.1)**/ 4935 (194.3)*	5020 (197.6)/ 5160 (203.1)**/ 4935 (194.3)*
Width	1820 (71.7)	1820 (71.7)/ 1828 (72.0)*	1820 (71.7)/ 1828 (72.0)*	1820 (71.7)/ 1828 (72.0)*	1820 (71.7)/ 1828 (72.0)*
Height	1437 (56.6)	1437 (56.6)/ 1441 (56.7)**	1437 (56.6)/1441 (56.7)**/1407 (55.4)	1437 (56.6)/ 1441 (56.7)**/ 1407 (55.4)	1442 (56.8)/ 1446 (56.9)**/ 1407 (55.4)*
Unladen weight – kg (lb)	1580 (3483)	1580 (3483)/ 1610 (3549)**	1700 (3748)/ 1730 (3814)**/ 1620 (3571)*	1770 (3902)/ 1800 (3968)**/ 1650 (3638)*	1830 (4034)/ 1860 (4101)**/ 1760 (3880)*
Units built	20,752	100,448/39,179**	13,815/70,935**/ 3461*	10,952/11,173**/ 6312*	1251/71,700**/ 26,791*

Note: data given is for European-specification models; 'Cat' denotes model fitted with catalytic converter.

A collection of detailed and beautifully illustrated books by Brian Long, covering a range of Mercedes-Benz models. Written by a highly regarded motoring writer, with many years' ownership of Mercedes cars behind him, these volumes provide the definitive study of each of these classic models. All variants and major world markets are looked at, along with competition history, and all lavishly illustrated with full colour photographs. Extensive appendices cover engine specifications, chassis numbers, build numbers and more.

Hardback • 25x25cm • colour pictures

For more information and price details, visit our website at www.veloce.co.uk
email: info@veloce.co.uk • Tel: +44(0)1305 260068